Oh No, We Forgot
to Have Children!

Oh No, We Forgot to Have Children!

How declining birth rates
are reshaping our society

Deirdre Macken

ALLEN&UNWIN

First published in 2005

Allen & Unwin
83 Alexander Street
Crows Nest NSW 2065
Australia
Phone: (61 2) 8425 0100
Fax: (61 2) 9906 2218
Email: info@allenandunwin.com
Web: www.allenandunwin.com

National Library of Australia
Cataloguing-in-Publication entry:

Macken, Deirdre.
   Oh no, we forgot to have children : how declining birth
   rates are reshaping our society.

   Includes index.
   ISBN 1 74114 477 9.

   1. Fertility, Human - Australia. 2. Childlessness - Social
   aspects - Australia. 3. Australia - Population. I. Title.

304.6320994

Set in 8/11 pt Quadraat-Regular by Bookhouse, Sydney
Printed by Griffin Press, South Australia

10 9 8 7 6 5 4 3 2 1

To all the children in my life.

Contents

Acknowledgments

I would like to thank my sister, Mary Macken Horarik, for her kind but rigorous reading; my other sisters, Wendy, Julie, Lucy and sister-in-law Beccy, for their support; and my parents Ann Daniel and Jim Macken for their constant encouragement and frequent reference support. I also thank Peter McDonald, Graeme Hugo, Robert Norman and Anne Clark, Carreen Leslie, Kerreen Reiger, Johanna Wyn, Graeme Russell and Leslie Cannold. Also the Australian Institute of Family Studies and the Australian Bureau of Statistics for their unfailing cheerful help. I should also thank Google. Most of all, I'd like to thank my family, Roger, Nicole, Kate and Toby for always being there for me and always encouraging my dreams.

Introduction

This book was driven by two events. One was a lunch, the other a book. The lunch was between three girlfriends, who'd started the same career full of brio, feminist ideas and ambition, and found themselves two decades later with six children between them and a few reservations about the choices they'd made. Should we have had more children? Should we have spent more time with our children? Did we give motherhood enough space in our lives? And then the challenge. Did we do enough for motherhood? Or, as Kate put it, 'We aren't doing enough to tell women about having children. We've told them about all the horror stories and nothing about the joy of children.'

Had we done enough for motherhood?

Her point rankled. What, I thought a few days later, had society done for us as mothers? We were the generation who had to remake ourselves as mothers. We'd left behind the 50s version of motherhood and stepped into a role that was largely ignored by our feminist sisters, barely tolerated by our bosses, patronised by our politicians and sidelined by the consumerist society. When we decided to have children, it was in spite of everything we had learned, everything that society was encouraging us to do and all economic wisdom. Motherhood in the 80s and 90s was the road less travelled. Each of us in our personal lives had seemed to be forging a new path. When is it a good time to have a baby? We'd talked about that through the years—one of us leaping into it, another taking a more considered approach, another leaving it late, almost too late. How much time does a child need with its mother? We'd debated the concept of 'quality time', the importance of mooching around with children and whether it's okay to feel bored when you're at home with a baby 24/7 and the greatest achievement of the day is to complete a cup of coffee. Individually we'd negotiated time off, part-time work, flexible work and refused a number of promotions that would have taken us up the career ladder. We'd conducted endless negotiations with partners about sharing the load, trying to find a compromise between the ideal of equality we'd learnt as feminists and the 50s landscape that informed our partners' ideas and, sometimes, our own ideas. We'd vacillated between the supermum, the soccer mum, working mum, the margarine mum and Mommy Dearest and felt relieved when we read that the good-enough mum was, well, good enough. As middle-class women, we'd battled to provide our children with what we thought they should have, without giving them everything we could have, while living in a society that told us that we should have it all. And, frankly, a lot of the journey was lonely, if only because we felt we had to be quiet about it.

For my generation of careerist mothers, motherhood was the elephant in the lounge room. We all knew how much of our time, energy and emotions mothering occupied but we kept this knowledge quiet. To our bosses, we pretended it was easy. We learnt to hide our status as mothers, to diminish the role that children played in our lives, and develop working schedules, lifestyles and attitudes that made light of our maternal roles. And in the process, we perpetrated the lie of modern motherhood—that it didn't dominate our lives that we could still perform at male breadwinner levels in our careers. No big deal.

We reserved our nightmares for other women. These stories were told around cafe tables and book clubs. They were stories about juggling work and home; the grief of sitting in an office with weeping breasts; the daily con of disappearing from the office at 5.30 p.m. while leaving a coat over the back of the chair; the guilt of sitting in emergency rooms with an ailing child while fielding work calls on the mobile. We told girlfriends horror stories about the wear and tear of birth, the vegetative mental state of pregnancy, the black hole of sleep deprivation and what happens to figures that don't get to the gym for a few years. We regaled them with tales of the family's fiscal black hole—the cost of child care, toys and then the cost of running a household with a few fashionable teenagers, the local takeaway on speed dial and a shower no one turns off properly.

We admitted our failures. I never made one Penelope Leach toy— even the one with cotton spools and string; I made packet cakes for the kindy cake stall; I sometimes felt relieved to go to work on Monday morning; I misdiagnosed a broken hand, made light of pneumonia and told an eight-year-old that a period was a full stop. But along the way we forgot to share enough of the good stories. Somehow, those Hallmark card pleasures such as watching a sleeping baby, catching the triumph of a baby taking her first steps, reading the first story she wrote about that well-trod trip to the beach passed without too much sharing. Our albums might have bulged with misty-eyed moments but our conversations too often skipped the Kodak details.

Years later, we sat at lunch wondering why women weren't having children. We were, at that late stage of our fertile lives, like war veterans sharing memories of an intense time of life. The passing of time had softened memories of the challenge; given a wider perspective than the view from the trenches; allowed us to think kindly of those who hadn't made it and wonder whether we'd done enough to promote peace. Perhaps, as veterans, we also allowed ourselves a sense of self-satisfaction. Or was that smugness? We'd done it, we'd taken the leap into motherhood, made the sacrifices and even if we didn't spend enough time mothering, we'd done our bit by our children, ourselves, our partners and, yes, Treasurer, by our country.

But had we done enough for motherhood?

The book that prompted further misgivings was called *The Coming Generational Storm*.[1] Much of this book concerns the economic consequences of the aging population, but it was the picture of the society just around the chronological corner that was the most disturbing. Our failure to reproduce ourselves and our cleverness at surviving is creating a century of the old. In Japan the average age will be 53 years within a few decades, in Europe it will be 52, in Australia the late 40s and even in a relatively fertile United States it will be 40-something. Countries like Japan and parts of Europe will start contracting within years and even Asian countries will struggle to replace themselves. The world we are creating will see more people wearing incontinence pads than babies wearing nappies; more in walking frames than in strollers; more park benches than adventure playgrounds. For the first time in human history, there will be more old people than young people.

The greying of the globe is the story of the increasing longevity of old age at one end of the demographic chart and the disappearance of children at the other end. For every man and woman to replace themselves, birth rates should be 2.1 babies per woman. Yet 59 countries have levels below replacement; 26 of the world's major countries have reported to the UN that they are worried about their low birth rate and the world population clock will start winding back within 50 years.

The prospect of living in an old world is difficult to imagine. What will happen to the vitality, pace and innovation of modern societies? Presumably it will be tempered—quashed?—by an older population's desire for safety, security and familiarity. Political and economic power will swing to older agendas; government policy will switch from expansion to managing contraction; environmentalists will be cleaning up ghost towns rather than trying to prevent shantytowns. The young may be treasured—if not for themselves, then for their economic contribution—or they might become prisoners of their own preciousness. Countries will vie for young workers; governments will force people into longer working lives and families with dependents will be mostly old women looking after ancient parents rather than young women nurturing babies. It's difficult to envisage the sort of world that is promised by those two-digit reproduction figures, if only because these demographic shifts are so new to us. It was only 30 years ago that the world was worrying about the population explosion and now demographers are warning of world population decline within the life of today's 30-year-olds. Even the expression 'baby boomer', that has dogged the lexicon since the soldiers returned home from World War II, has given the impression that population is still more of a boom than a bust. Perhaps it will take a generation called baby busters for most to realise that if current population trends continue, the world will end not with a bang but a whimper.

How did the world forget to have children?

Somewhere between the lunch with friends and the book on demography lay the story of modern motherhood and the future of society. All around the industrialised world those cafe conversations between women, the bedtime chats between couples and the quiet debates that a woman has with herself are remaking our personal lives and the future of the planet.

The story of the baby bust—both personal and global—is largely a tale about women and, in particular, all the things that have impacted on women's desire and ability to be mothers. It starts with the contraceptive pill in the 60s, it's shaped by feminism in the 70s but it's also a factor of media culture, economic opportunities, rampant capitalism, biological advances, the changing shape of family and a materialistic society. While there are variations within different countries, there is much commonality in the reasons why an Italian woman will end up childless, an Australian woman will end up with one child and an American soccer mom will settle for two.

Throughout this book, I have looked at why women have children or why they don't. It primarily addresses women because while men can, and do, decide not to have children, men can't decide to have them. It is still women who must make the final decision and there are many more options for women to have a child with or without a partner. Having said this, the role of men as fathers is a key consideration in the debate.

At the heart of modern motherhood is the issue of choice. Since there has been effective contraception, women have technically been able to choose children or not. Since women's greater participation in the workforce, women have had more economic freedom to choose children or not. Since the feminist revolution, women have been able to choose social roles that may include motherhood or may not. It is the element of choice that is changing the shape of motherhood and society. The old presumption that women will always have kids, that outside a few blimps like war or depression, women will get down to the business of having babies no longer holds true. In today's society women don't 'instinctively' have children, they look at the world around them and then make choices. Many are voting with their wombs. This is women's choice and their choices are saying something about society's failure, because a society that chooses not to replace itself is a sick society. By definition, a society that continues to choose not to replace itself will die out. Later rather than sooner, the last Adam and Eve will be left standing and they too might decide it's not worth the bother.

Of course, some women don't get to make those choices. Women who miss the biological boat or don't have partners at the right time or the right partners at the right time or who break up with partners before completing their family will experience fertility as a disappointment. The same trends that give choices to women— biological technology, economic freedom and wider roles in society—sometimes conspire to distract or discourage women from the idea of motherhood. One day, some of them will turn around and say, oh no, I forgot to have children.

In exploring the landscape that forms the backdrop of women's decisions, I have attempted to cover the social, cultural, political, economic, historic and philosophical factors that influence a woman's choices. In this pop sociologist's approach I've relied on academic texts, interviews, talk-back radio transcripts, statistics, chick lit books, television series, speeches, budget papers, media reports, polls and personal recollections. It is inevitably not just a woman's perspective, but that of a middle-class urban woman living in the developed world.

I also polled my alma mater on the eve of our 30th reunion to get a snapshot of how the class of 74 had fared at the new frontier of reproduction. Now that they were at the end of their fertile lives, I wondered how many had had children, whether they'd had as many as they wanted, at what age they'd had them and whether they'd do it all again. Of the 38 who replied to my highly selective poll, the average fertility was 2.5 children—slightly higher than that achieved by most women their age (several had not had children, one had had ten). However, if they had their time again, most would have had more children (except for the one with ten). On average they would have three children, if they could do it again. Perhaps the most consistent story of those women was that most had had children later than they had planned, and some much later. More than half said they'd had them late, several had children in their forties and five had sought assistance with fertility—one was still trying for a child at the age of 47. The responses gave snapshots of lives that, when read together, formed something of an album for that group of women who stepped out of a middle-class education into a world that would change beneath their feet. Their comments, which appear throughout this book, had a recurring theme of surprise. For most of them, things hadn't turned out the way they were planned, or the way they presumed they would. It was obvious that not many of them had had 'the family they always wanted'. That idea used to be an assumption of young women, now it's only a minority of older mothers who can say they had the family they wanted.

Through this media kaleidoscope of personal and political, academic and anecdote, it's possible to catch glimpses not just of how much motherhood has changed but how relationships have changed, how families are evolving and how the next generation is likely to parent. There are indications too of how our view of ourselves as biological beings is being reshaped by fertility technology; that the haphazard nature of procreation is being replaced by a timetable, a presumption that we can all have a child whenever we want it. It's the consumer's approach to biology—I'll have a brown-eyed boy with a sprinkle of freckles, hold the tantrums. And as mothering changes, childhood too morphs into something that increasingly resembles a working life. The childhood of billy-carts that occupies the society imagination has been replaced by a childhood of institutions, timetables and value-adding programs.

The fertility debate is one where the personal has become political—on a global scale. As demography becomes the political issue of the 21st century, it is in the realm of the personal that the future is made, or unmade. The economic and social impact of our personal decisions will force a rethink by governments on the role of the family but it's also a chance for all of us to rethink the role of family in our lives. However, discussions about procreation that revert to a white picket fence view of the world are doomed to failure—indeed, that is one of the reasons for women opting out of the classic family role.

We live in rational times. We approach our own fertility with technological know-how. We run a measuring tape over our homes and think of the real estate price. We engineer lifestyles that mimic time-motion studies and adopt the language of management to describe them. We multi-task, allot quality time, manage households, monitor our diets and tick off experiences. Yet having children is an irrational decision. It is a leap into love, a dice with destiny, a wade through the swamp of emotions and a commitment to nurture until the end no matter what challenges or disappointments arise. Having children and spending time with children is a daily reconnection with our human core in a world that would prefer to downsize that part of us.

A year after that lunch with my friends, I'm still bemused by how bothered I was by that comment—what have we done for mother-hood? Yes, part of it was frustration: what had society ever done for us as mothers! But on reflection, I think there was also some guilt (a hardy perennial of motherhood). Maybe we had helped diminish the role of motherhood in society by downplaying it in our personal lives. If loudmouths like me had spoken up about the importance of motherhood, it might have a higher status in society and a higher priority in personal lives. Maybe a few nappy flags, pram blockades and burnt maternity bras might have put mothering on the national agenda. We seemed to be apologising for everything, when we should have been demanding. We put 'Baby on Board' stickers on the windscreen and expected others to care. We were grateful for scraps off the economic table, when we should have fronted up with our bowls and asked for more. Also I think there was some fear in my response. As the mother of two daughters, I began to wonder what sort of personal and social legacy of mothering had been left to them. They're growing up in a world that is increasingly devoid of children, in economic systems that are anti-children and with memories of a mother who was often conflicted and sometimes cranky. There's a better way to do motherhood and, as an optimist, I think they'll find it. But they are going to need support and, as a society, we can't afford to refuse them this support.

My friends and I are at the tail end of our reproductive lives but whenever a young friend or family member asks about having a child, I feel I can only tell them that there's never a good time to have children—much less a perfect time—but I've never met a mother who regrets having children and I've met too many women who say they forgot to have children. As one of my old school friends said in response to the poll, 'You are assuming our child-bearing years are over. They may be for some but not for me!' There should be more that I can say to my friends, my children and to my old school friend. Perhaps this is the start.

The future is the past

If demography is destiny, then a trip to one of the least fertile places in the world offers a peek into our future. In 2003, I visited the Spanish town of Bilbao with my eldest daughter, Nicole, who was eighteen years old. On the second day we were there, she stopped in the middle of a cobbled street and declared, 'This place is so old!' To which, I replied, 'It's Europe, it's meant to be old.'

She wasn't referring to the age of the cobbled streets. 'It's the people,' she said, 'all the people are old.' I hadn't noticed but later that day a civic official I was interviewing told me that the birth rate of Bilbao was 0.8, the lowest in Europe, little more than a third of the rate of 2.1 which is needed to maintain a stable population. For the next few days I viewed the town through the eyes of Nicole and that statistic. The streets were quiet, well mannered, business-like. Except for people in the tapas bars in the ancient quarters, the nights were sparsely populated. It took us two days to see some children. And that was a sobering sight. We were in parkland in the middle of the town where a child's playground adjoined a museum. In the late morning, grandparents, dressed in Sunday best, steered prams slowly along pathways towards the playground. None had more than one child in tow and the children were dressed as well as their grandparents. It was like an outing from a nineteenth-century novel of manners. In the playground nine or ten adults—both grandparents and parents—surrounded half a dozen toddlers and preschoolers. There were almost two adults to every child. Even allowing for more formal European manners, these children were being treated like treasures—rare and endangered. And perhaps a little difficult to handle. By the time we left the museum, the playground was near empty.

As someone born in the baby boom, I remember parks full of children but virtually devoid of adults. In the 50s and 60s, tribes of children would descend on parks, often with younger brothers and sisters in tow. They'd make the swings, trees, slides and and bushland their own domain, their own fantasyland. The sight of these single, precious children in Bilbao accompanied by hovering adults was like visiting a museum and seeing a glass display cabinet of childhood— Please Do Not Touch the Exhibits. I didn't realise it then, but the ratio of ages in the playground was a preview of the world we will soon be living in. We are building a world where the old will outnumber the young for the first time in human history. Whereas today, children under the age of fourteen outnumber the over-60s by three to one, within 50 years there will be more old people than children.[1] Moreover, according to UN estimates, the ratio will be far worse in developed countries, like Spain, where there will be twice as many old people as children. There will be many grandparents but they won't have many grandchildren to take to the park.

The science of demographics enables us to paint a picture of the future. Birth rates are the template for tomorrow's society. They are a foundation stone that can be chipped away through death and moved around the globe but can never be expanded. It's difficult to envisage the landscape of the future through discussion of such tiny numbers and such seemingly small shifts in these numbers. But the impact over time is astounding. A birth rate of just below replacement—1.9—means that over a century a country's population will fall to 82 per cent of its original size without immigration. In Australia, with a current population of 20 million, that would mean a population of 16.4 million by the end of the 21st century. However, with a fertility rate of 1.3, the population would fall to a quarter of its original size. In Australia that would mean a population of five million within 100 years—the number of Australians there were during World War I. The current fertility rate of just above 1.7 would erode the population by almost 50 per cent over the century, if it weren't alleviated by immigration. The country that lived by the principle 'populate or perish' for most of its white history, would be half the size in the space of one person's life—a centenarian's life span at least. At present, most countries in the developed world have birth rates of between 1 and 1.9, so large parts of Europe, Asia and Australia are heading for a diminished future, unless they ramp up their immigration. The map of the world is being redrawn right now and for those with low fertility and little immigration, the landscape will have fewer people, fewer towns, abandoned farms, empty houses, shuttered shops and quiet parks.

As a society, we're breeding for extinction. At the end of 2003, the Liberal Party's Malcolm Turnbull told a University of NSW audience, 'At the peak of our technological achievement, the Western world appears to have lost the will to reproduce itself. Great cultures like Italy, Spain, Greece and Japan (to name but four) could become functionally extinct within a century.'[2]

Turnbull, along with some demographers, went on to reach back into the history of plagues to describe the impact of this collapse. As Barbara Tuchman says in *A Distant Mirror*, the plagues of Europe in the fourteenth century wiped out a third of the population and turned large, thriving towns into ghost towns, which are now only discernible by regular shaped mounds in the countryside. She writes:

> *The obvious and immediate result of the Black Death was, of course, a shrunken population, which owing to wars, brigandage and recurrence of the plague, declined even further by the end of the 14th century. It eventually receded, leaving Europe with a population reduced by about 40 per cent in 1380 and by nearly 50 per cent at the end of the century.*

Interestingly, Tuchman notes that one of the longer-term consequences of the plague was something that is already troubling world leaders today—the need to raise taxes when there aren't enough workers or production to support society's needs. 'The vanishing of taxable material caused rulers to raise rates of taxation, arousing resentment that was to explode in repeated outbreaks in coming decades',[3] she writes.

Throughout history, wars have wreaked havoc on population profiles—ethnic cleansing has devastated populations of Jews, Muslims, African tribes, Armenians and various other European ethnic groups. The toll of war has carved into populations of young men. War has also caused hiccups in birth rates both during and after war, a dearth of babies during the crisis and a recovery of families afterwards.

The 21st-century demographic challenge takes babies from society, not soldiers or the sick. It might not produce bodies to bury, but it leaves a great absence in our families and communities and a great hole in our future; it will make many small towns disappear and with them, their history, culture and possibly their language. Perhaps if the baby bust did leave bodies in the street, we might be more concerned. Instead, the slow disappearance of youth is more likely to have us commenting on how picturesque and quiet the parks are; after a while, we get used to the peace and quiet and begin to think that that's the way parks should be. A few years ago in my neighbourhood, there were moves to limit children's access to one of the playing fields that were regularly used by adult cricket teams. The sporting association argued that the adult team was very successful, they took practice seriously and the continual presence of children was upsetting the turf and the timetable for adult players. The sporting group was unsuccessful but no one thought to ask them where they'd get their future players if they barred children from the playing field.

The absence of children in modern societies is a demographic death knell, one that we should have heard years ago. It is the most powerful message that people could send to their leaders. The text of that message would spell out that there was something wrong with the system if people are writing themselves out of the future. That we didn't hear it, or heed it, owes something to the population explosion which threatened to overwhelm the world's resources in the 60s and 70s. That explosion in numbers was partly due to an increase in birth rates and partly due to a decrease in death rates. In Asia especially, infant mortality declined and better health increased the life span of the elderly. But even as the spectre of a population explosion was gaining currency, the reality was changing. By the end of the 60s, contraception was dampening fertility in the developed world and was moving into undeveloped regions. Most adults today still think the population explosion is still happening, at least in Asia. It isn't. In several developed countries of Asia, the birth rate is below replacement.

With the exception of wars and plagues, population graphs tend to maintain a pyramid shape. There are many babies and children down at the bottom of the graph and numbers taper off at the top as ages rise. A century ago, Australia's population pyramid had a solid base of children. The birth rate hovered between 3.7 and 4 children per woman in the first decade of the twentieth century, but it declined steadily over the following two decades and during the Depression it stood at 2.1—the replacement level. It's obvious that even without modern contraception women have been able to exercise some control on the number of children they bear. It helps if their menfolk are away at war or hitting the road in search of jobs. Nevertheless, there is a long history of association between social and economic conditions and birth rates. However, it was modern contraception that took reproduction out of biology and placed it solidly in the land of society, culture and economics. The birth rate soared after the end of World War II and reached its modern era peak of 3.5 babies per woman in 1961—the high tide of the baby boom. In May 1960, the US Federal Drug Administration gave approval for the pill that had been marketed for 'menstrual disorders' to be sold as the birth control pill. Within a year, there were one million American users, within five years there were six million women on the pill. The impact in Australia was just as dramatic. When oral contraception became available, the birth rate dropped from 3.5 to 2.9 in just five years from 1961 to 1966—and continued to decline throughout the 70s. Replacement level—2.1—was reached in 1976 but the decline didn't stop. With the impact of feminism, better education opportunities for women and the expansion of the workforce in the 80s and 90s, the rate continued to erode. In 1990, it was still at a relatively healthy 1.9 but over the decade it fell to its present rate of roughly 1.7 births. Australia's overall population continued to increase during those three decades of below-replacement reproduction largely because of an escalation in the immigration program and the impact of those baby boomers producing their own children.

Australia's story was echoed around the developed world. However, the impact of the baby strike was greater in countries with little or no immigration, in countries with patriarchal family and social traditions.

In the next few decades, more of the population pyramids around the world will invert. The foundation for those pyramids will look wobbly, there will literally be fewer young people supporting the upper echelons of old. Demographers refer to this as the 'coffin' shape of population. For good reason.

In Europe, there will be 20 per cent fewer citizens within 50 years: the Ukraine will lose 40 per cent of its current population and Russia will see a 28 per cent decline, from 140 million to just over 100 million. The world's population will stabilise at nine billion in the next 40 years and some predict that by the end of this century there will be 500 million fewer people living on the planet. The momentum for extinction—at least of towns and countryside—is already under way. In fact, demographers refer to Europe as having a negative momentum. That is, even if the next generation of women boost the birth rate back to replacement level, populations will continue to shrink because there are fewer women of child-bearing age coming through.

The future of the world is being written now. What's more, it's not being decided in the White House, or in corporate headquarters, in think tanks, religious doctrines or in a laboratory somewhere. This future is being decided in bedrooms across the world. In the privacy of their bedroom (let's be conservative here), couples decide whether to have a baby this year or next, or when the mortgage has been reduced, or not at all. Couples with one child juggle with the decision about having another—soon, so there won't be two disruptions to their earning capacity, or much later when they're not so exhausted, or maybe not at all. Privately, single women wrestle with their options—is it too late, will they find a partner on time, should they conceive without a partner? And many more women are asking why they should risk their career, independence and the freedom to travel for a life constrained by children.

It is these quiet conversations that are redrawing the map of tomorrow's world. And it is possible to trace some of these personal decisions into demographic figures. The most obvious manifestation of low birth numbers is the increase in childlessness. Today, one in five Australian women who are at the end of their child-bearing years have not had children and this is expected to rise to one in four women if trends continue. The middle-aged childless woman is the image of the low-births debate. She appears in media stories, she writes of the experience, she's the prototype. But while the doubling in the incidence of childlessness over the last few decades is significant, the biggest impact on the statistics is the scaling down of families. Basically, those who do decide to have families are having smaller families than they did in previous generations. They're also having smaller families than they thought they would when they were younger. It's not so much, 'Honey, I shrank the kids', but 'Honey, I shrank the family'. Those who might have had two children in the past, or who wanted two children, are often settling for one child or are just ending up with one child. Those who would have had three or four or even five children are having two, maybe three. The big family, which was still quite common a generation ago, virtually doesn't exist today. One-third of women who were born in 1930 went on to have four or more children. Thirty years later, only 12 per cent of women born in 1960 have had four or more. Those who have large families are both statistical and social freaks. When I told friends and colleagues that I was expecting my third child, I encountered much surprise, bemusement and a little bit of anger. Wasn't I a career woman? Had I gone back to Catholicism? Didn't I want a life? Did I really fancy driving a people mover? Hadn't I fixed my problems with contraception? Does this mean you'll have a fourth? And the most common reaction—I suppose you're trying for a boy. I let most of them think that I was trying for a boy, if only because I couldn't adequately explain why I wanted to have three children. I wanted a bit of a tribe, a rumble in the house; to me, a family was where the kids outnumbered the adults and, I suppose, I liked the other two so much I wanted another. In a society of downsizing families, my decision to have a third child entailed a black mark on my CV, an appointment with a car dealer and a place at the slightly whacky end of the demographic scale.

Obviously, not many women choose to have large families today but the reasons why the average size of the family has contracted so much are also tied to women's delay in starting families. Australian National University demographer Peter McDonald, in a paper titled, 'Low Fertility: Unifying the theory and the demography', has found that relatively low birth rates—between 1.5 and 2 babies per woman—are tied to postponing child-bearing.[4] That is, women are putting off starting families to a later age because they are spending more time in education, more time in the workforce and they are partnering later. Whereas a woman who starts a family at the age of 25 has roughly ten fertile years in which to have a few children, a woman who starts at 30 has only five or six years to have children, and someone who starts at 35 will often find it hard to have one child.

Some of my old school friends experienced this time crunch of late starting families.

Frankly, I wasn't ready to settle down and have a family until my mid-thirties when I had achieved an education, worked etc. While I would have loved more children, I think I was lucky to have two—born when I was 34 and 39. Clearly, my fertility was dropping, if that is the correct expression, but I couldn't think of anything worse than having to study and have children at the same time. I could not have coped or enjoyed either. I was lucky for the way things worked out except for the fact that I missed out on having a bigger family.

Another comments that her family of two was dictated by a late start.

I had my first child at 34, so if I'd started earlier, I might have considered having another one. Interestingly, although I had my children relatively late, I was still one of the first of my close group of friends to have children, that is, of the ones who've had children at all.

It's worth remembering that most couples still want to have children. Surveys by the Australian Institute of Family Studies, have consistently shown that in their early twenties, the average person very much wants to have a child and expects to have a child (women more so than men).[5] However, as they age, their expectations of having children decline although their desire for children usually hangs in there longer. But even when a woman is in her late thirties, she'll rate her desire for a child at five out of ten even though her expectations are just three out of ten. When you look at the graphs of desires and expectations, and the growing gap between them, it's obvious that something is awry. Around the world, couples that had once imagined having a clan are resigning themselves to 'just the two'—a family foreclosed early. Millions of women who had envisaged raising a couple of children now have a single child. And millions of other women and men approaching the end of their fertile lives—often brilliant, creative and fulfilled people in every other way—now realise that their family will always be in the past. For the childless, family is their history, not their future.

As McDonald says:

> *Young people, in the main, do not graduate from their families of origin and from the education system with low fertility preferences. A preference for two children remains dominant among women and men in the early twenties. This means that very low fertility is more a product of constraint than of preference. Aside from the macroeconomic disadvantages of very low fertility, the frustration of people's preferences to have children does not make for a healthy society. Indeed, wealthy societies in which fertility is very low can be seen as abrogating the human rights of their citizens.*[6]

Just as the Black Death left an empty landscape in its wake, the epidemic of childlessness and downsized families will reconfigure the landscape of tomorrow.

On our travels through Spain and Portugal, I had a glimpse of how the maps of habitation are being redrawn in these areas of very low fertility. A train trip through the heart of Portugal exposed many market gardens that had been abandoned. The towns we spied from the window of the train seemed curiously empty, except for the odd woman hanging washing from windows. In the inland cities, the plazas were full of old men, smoking and chatting on corners. No, they weren't that old, they were in their fifties and sixties but they clearly didn't have anything else to do with their day. At times, we saw a toddler appear to chase pigeons around the plaza and after school hours we saw small groups of school children making their way home, but these were fleeting impressions.

After two weeks on the road it struck me that my children are already experiencing a world community that is very different from the one I knew. The landscape of the world is older for them, the nights are quieter, the afternoons disappear into siesta, the pigeons in the park are well fed but the playgrounds are emptier, the cafes are sleepy, the street sounds are muted. As they grow into their era, my children will find like-minded communities but they'll find it in pockets of the globe rather than everywhere they go. There aren't many indicators of a place's vitality, no geiger counters of human activity, but youth pick that up intuitively. Nicole could tell long before I could, that the streets of Bilbao were old. Her generation will continue to suss out the places in the world where they feel at home and those where they feel caught in a time warp from someone else's era. And we'll miss them when they're gone.

The bionic woman

When my partner and I decided to have a child—and isn't that phrase presumptuous—I thought I'd keep a note of my cycles so the obstetrician could work out my due date. Early in 1983, I wrote the date on a strip of notepaper and tucked it into my wallet so I could pull it out when I made my first visit. Next month I wrote down another date. Then another and another. Winter arrived and left. Spring came and left. My dates had got to the bottom of the paper when I started to wonder just how presumptuous I'd been.

My generation was the first to approach parenthood with a date in mind. By the time we were teenagers, the pill was available even to those without a ring on their left hand, abortion had been taken out of the back alleys and IUDs, even if not safe, at least did the job. It was hard to imagine how our mothers coped with the knowledge that they could 'fall' pregnant because of a wonky cycle, a miscalculation of dates or a moment of unbridled (and unsheathed) passion. Their daily lives had an undercurrent of watchfulness, at any one time they were aware of where they stood in the flows of their fertility cycles. They would have greeted the arrival of their period with some emotion, whether it was quiet relief or disappointment or a bit of both. In the days before reliable contraception, fertility was a constant presence in women's lives and, whether they liked it or not, women were in touch with their monthly rhythms.

For my generation, family planning meant contraception. Even the Family Planning Association, whose name suggests it might have something to do with getting a family started, was thought of as the place you went to get the pill without questions, for advice on abortions or to sort out problems with IUDs. No one I knew went to a clinic to get advice on having babies. We only noticed fertility when we crossed over to the other side, when we decided we wanted to become pregnant. And after years of being free from pregnancy, many weren't prepared for the random nature of fecundity. It's only when a woman throws away contraception that she faces the question—will she be able to have children? Even women who've been pregnant before but not proceeded with it, don't know whether their fertility has survived the ordeal or the years. Facing that first natural cycle is a moment of hope and fear. And with each cycle that subsequently passes, there is less hope and more fear.

After a few months of noting dates, I began to investigate. I counted the days between dates and analysed the cycles. Aren't they meant to be all the same length? I began taking my temperature to pinpoint days of ovulation—just like Sheila Kitzinger said. But my temperature was all over the place, especially on sleep-in Sundays. Briefly I thought about the Billings method—a way of telling when you're ovulating that is mostly used to avoid pregnancy. But then I remembered all those Catholic families that had used the Billings method—those BIG Catholic families. In the months I spent trying to figure out what was happening on that scrap of paper, I'd entered the modern story of fertility—the quest to control the process of fertility, pregnancy, birth and child-rearing.

Some time over the last 40 years there has been a shift in our notions of controlling fertility. We no longer just expect medical technology to prevent us getting pregnant; we expect it to provide a pregnancy. The generation that grew up knowing that they wouldn't fall pregnant unless they wanted to, now presume they'll be able to do so whenever and whatever it takes. My track down the technological highway ended just after the ninth date when a pink line appeared on a pregnancy test (signalling the early days of a brown-eyed girl with ringlets and a penchant for singing at dawn). But for many women today the decision to get pregnant is the start of a journey that takes them away from ancient approaches to procreation into the clinics of technology.

The management of biology has been the liberation of women but it's meant that the decision to have a child is now a rational decision. Couples are supposed to plan parenthood. They are expected to choose the right time to start a family, then they have to figure out when and if to have a second and then they have to make a decision about whether they want any more children. For the two-career, urban couple there are many things to factor into their decision. Ideally, the education bills should be cleared, careers should be on track or have reached a certain level, the mortgage should be under control, the travel bug should have passed, renovations should be completed, they should have agreed in principle on child-rearing plans and on matters of religion and schooling. This clear-minded approach was mentioned by one of my school colleagues in her response to a questionnaire.

I think the cost of raising kids these days is a definite reason for parents to choose to have less children. This cost is in both the energy you put into raising them and the dollars spent. I also think that there are so many additional things available to both parents and children today that having too many children can impinge on these.

This shift to choice was the dream of our feminist mothers. We finally have control of our biology. A child is the choice of a couple not the offspring of an accident. But rationality can also be a trap. What seems rational for our economic situations and lifestyles isn't always what is sensible for our biological selves. There's a growing disconnection between the reality of biology and our idea of what our bodies are capable of; between the time we want to have children and the time when our bodies are best at having children.

As the head of Adelaide University's Reproductive Medicine Unit, Robert Norman, said in an interview for this book, 'What we're doing is moving the desired fertility age into the biologically inappropriate age'.[1]

The exquisite agony that couples often go through when they place the question of children on the table has been fictionalised in Amanda Lohrey's 2004 book, The Philosopher's Doll. Kirsten, 36, wants a baby. Her partner, Lindsay, isn't sure and as a philosopher he can extrapolate all the reasons why they shouldn't have a baby—yet. They may have a two-storey Edwardian house but the mortgage is still large, the renovations are not yet complete, he likes eating out, sleeping in and making love spontaneously on Saturday afternoon. Besides, he says, she's only 36.[2] The book elegantly tours between economic man, who is bound by his rationality, and emotional woman, who is bound to an impending biological bomb. That throwaway comment of his—she's only 36—lies at the heart of so many personal tragedies and society's looming fertility crisis.

The delay in starting families is a key reason for declining fertility rates in the developed world. This isn't just because more women are leaving it so late that they discover fertility problems or break up with their partner before they get around to having children. It's mainly because the later a woman starts a family, the fewer children she will be able to fit into the remaining window of opportunity. In the final two decades of the twentieth century the median age at which Australian women had first children rose from 26 years to 30 years and the percentage of women who were childless at their 30th birthday rose from 35 per cent to 60 per cent. The proportion of births to women over the age of 40 rose from less than 1 per cent to 3 per cent. And that last figure shouldn't give the primigravida too much comfort, according to Robert Norman. Late motherhood does happen, but with only three out of 100 babies being born to women of 40-plus, it's still more headline stuff than everyday stuff.

'Women still think they're highly fertile in their forties,' says Robert Norman.

One survey asked them what they thought their chances of having a baby at the age of 45 was and most said 50 per cent, whereas it is less than 1 per cent. The rare women who have kids in their mid-forties—Cherie Blair, Madonna—are role models for people. They think it can happen, so it will probably be all right. But when we look at natural fertility patterns in groups that don't use contraceptives—the Hutterites in the US for instance—you see that fertility drops off very rapidly from 36 onwards and, indeed, at 38 fertility rates are half those of the early to mid-twenties. You should also remember that the frequency of intercourse decreases with age so not only does your chance of getting pregnant each time diminish but the number of opportunities diminishes.[3]

This idea that fertility is a linear event that begins at puberty and tracks right up to menopause is widespread despite recent warnings from fertility experts. As most of the these experts say, many women think they are almost as fertile when they approach menopause as they are in their twenties. A survey of 300 undergraduate students at the University of Western Australia showed a sunny outlook among those who've yet to see how restricted the window is. Seven out of ten described themselves as highly fertile and most said they would delay having children because of careers or lifestyles and, if they hit trouble later, then IVF would come to their rescue.[4]

One of my school friends, who almost missed her opportunity to have a child, pointed to the difficulty of reminding youth that nothing—especially not biology—lasts forever.

> If I had my time again, I would like to think I would be more educated about how your eggs age etc etc. Though it's hard to know if you can really warn young career girls in their 20s how hard it could be to get pregnant later when and if they meet Mr Right.

Young women and men who like to think that IVF is there to pick up after busy careers and busted relationships are the sort of people who end up in Norman's reproductive medicine unit and they might be in for a disappointment. 'There's this belief that IVF is a safety net, especially if you get to 45 and are still unsuccessful, yet IVF is a spectacularly unsuccessful intervention at that age. It's basically hopeless without donor eggs.' Another fertility expert, Robert Jansen, medical director of Sydney IVF, has also attempted to correct the idea that technology can rescue the dreams of older would-be mothers. In the late 90s the average age of women seeking IVF was 39 and yet Jansen's research has shown that 39 is six years too late for a reasonable outcome. In a survey of 565 women who visited the clinic, he found that up to the age of 34 years women had a 52 per cent chance of a live birth with IVF. But, 'after 33 years there is an almost unremitting, linear decline in fertility to reach zero at 45 years', he says. There's also a sharp increase in miscarriages, from 10 per cent for under-35-year-olds, to 16 per cent for those in their late thirties and up to 43 per cent for the over-forties.[5]

The news that the fertility window is smaller than imagined—stretching little more than fifteen years after a woman's 21st birthday—is especially hard to grasp in an era when all other life stages are getting longer. The period of adolescence, or adulescence as some refer to it, now lasts till the late twenties, with youth staying in education longer, travelling the world, dropping in and out of jobs and living at home longer. The other end of life is also elongating. The period after retirement was just a few years in the early part of the twentieth century, but today the new retiree can expect to live for a few decades in retirement. Even middle age has stretched into a long twilight that starts at about age 40 and goes to the late sixties.

Against these elongated life stages, it seems cruel to be told that the fertility window of opportunity is small, tighter than most imagined and that even technology won't make it much bigger. Moreover, those 30-something-year-olds who have remained fit and healthy find it hard to believe that their reproductive fitness is not as good as their well-honed abdominal muscles. When many 30-something-year-olds can still look like a 20-something-year-old, run marathons like an East African and have a diet rich in sushi, it's hard to convince them that their ovaries and testes aren't as easily buffed to perfection. Flick through the magazine media and see how many late-life mothers comment on how their path to motherhood was paved by yoga, or an organic diet or the right attitude. Luck and a lot of sex maybe, but the ability to do a downward dog pose has never been linked with a successful journey to the delivery suite. Tests are now being introduced that allow women to check their reproductive age—that is, check the viability of their store of eggs.[6] These tests were developed from research that found it's not so much your chronological age that's important but how far away you are from menopause. Fertility falls off rapidly twelve to fourteen years before menopause—on average this occurs at about the age of 37, but it will be much earlier or later depending on when that woman is destined to go through menopause. Some women at 40 may be only 32 in reproductive years but some other 40-year-olds may be 48 in reproductive years. For a few women who are destined to enter early menopause, their fertility would be compromised by the age of 30.

The concept that reproductive biology can be managed, scheduled, manipulated, ramped up and switched on and off as many times as you want is understandable given the sort of information in the media. What we learn about the end stage of fertility is conducted in a different classroom to where we learnt about the start of reproduction. Most adults today went to PD sessions at school where they learnt about menstrual cycles, unexplained damp spots in boys' beds and the remarkable tenacity of sperm wiggling through the ova wall. But few were told that all this wiggling and tracking down tubes had a finite life, that sperm would become weak swimmers and the egg would have trouble getting through to the uterus and that this crotchety middle age of sperm and ova would begin sooner than we thought . . . The vibrant start of our fertile lives was taught in the classrooms and, whether we listened or threw spitballs at the ceiling, it was the foundation of our views on reproduction. The dying stage of our fertility is a more modern focus and discussion of it is left largely in the hands of news media and book publishing.

An informal survey conducted among the patients of the Sydney clinic, Fertility First, found that half the people seeking help had got their information on fertility from family and friends, 20 per cent got information from literature and only 30 per cent from their GPs. As the medical director of the clinic Anne Clark says, 'Your family and friends aren't going to have up to date information on fertility and they won't necessarily have accurate information'. She's found that more informed patients tend to have overly pessimistic views of their chances but the less informed 'come in expecting this will happen and they can't understand why it's not going to happen straightaway, especially in an IVF setting. When it doesn't happen immediately, they presume you've done something wrong, rather than this is what reproduction is like for humans.' Two of the most common misconceptions about fertility technology, Clark says, revolve around how long a couple should wait before getting assistance and the fact that 50 per cent of fertility problems are male problems.[7]

A quick trawl through newspaper files on the subject of fertility reveals that headlines are not the source for balanced or comprehensive information on the subject. Here's a precis of some of the headlines over the past few years:

Study Finds Women Can Give Birth at 70. Older Mothers Still Have the Stomach to Deliver the Goods. Monkey Success Offers Hope for Infertile Women. Dead Sperm Donors Now True Fathers. Eggs in the Lab, And Bob's Your Mother.

The news media is always attuned to the new, the bizarre and shocking but these headlines nevertheless infiltrate readers' views. With such amazing science happening on a regular basis, one can only conclude that technology has surpassed biology. Our bodies may let us down but science will rescue us.

Browsing through books in the local library will further reassure us. *Your Pregnancy After 35*, *Midlife Motherhood*, *Birth Begins at 40: Challenging the myths about late motherhood* and *The Fastest Way to get Pregnant Naturally* were just a few in my local library. Again the impression is that if there's a manual for it, it must be doable.

Even the language of the fertility industry gives an inflated reassurance to those relying on a technological rescue for their baby dreams. The word 'barren' no longer appears anywhere in relation to childless women. This forlorn word with all its associations of uselessness and lifelessness has fortunately slipped from the lexicon. (Worth noting it was never used to describe men without offspring.) Women are also rarely referred to as 'infertile'; instead they have 'fertility problems' and that implies not an end to the discussion, but the start of a challenge. A problem is something to overcome and the fertility industry has an ever-widening repertoire of treatments to treat the problem. Moreover, the range of these treatments and their techie names create the impression that the experts have things under control for us. Log on to any fertility site and you'll find references to intra cytoplasmic sperm injection, frozen embryos, interuterine insemination, gamete intra fallopian transfer, preimplantation genetic diagnosis, ovary-stimulating pills, ovulation monitoring and gestational surrogates. It sounds like the sort of thing you'd hear at a NASA space launch. At the very least, it sounds as if we've got all the bases covered. Somewhere in that list is a product that must be right for us. A bit of a tickle of the ovary, a quick squirt of sperm in the right spot and . . . we have lift-off!

With such a range of off-the-shelf reproduction, it's not surprising that many bring a consumer mindset to the process of having babies. Many of those couples who queue outside Robert Norman's unit have done their homework and their sums by the time they get there. He states:

The reason people are leaving it later is a combination of them feeling that they're going to be fine because others have achieved it in their early forties but there's also a blindness caused by the economic imperatives that couples face. This blocking off is also a male problem. It's the men who usually don't want to have children too early and they're the ones who advance all the economic imperatives that delay it.

When I counsel couples about IVF, it's the man who's concerned about the money. When we talk about the number of embryos to put back, we spend a lot of time talking about the fact that putting two back has a high chance of producing twins and having twins is not the ideal outcome. But the guy will always say, that's fine, I'll go for it because it will be cheaper to do on one cycle whereas the women are more concerned about the outcome for the baby.[8]

Another fertility expert, Stephen Steigrad of the (Sydney) Royal Hospital for Women's Department of Reproductive Medicine, voiced his frustration with the children of 1971 who were then approaching the critical years of fertility. In a *Sydney Morning Herald* story in 2003, Steigrad said: 'They feel as though they are immortal, so why would they worry about having kids? They are all out there getting themselves organised with the basics: two Beamers in the garage, every whitegood in creation, plasma screen TV. They are saying: "We can't possibly have a child yet".' He added that infertility would probably be this generation's first career disaster.[9]

Many of our misconceptions about fertility unfold at the clinics that are now a major feature of the health system. A medical field that was largely experimental and based in universities just twenty years ago is now an industry with production line systems, large turnovers and a customer base that grows annually.

Fertility First in Sydney's western suburbs is one of the independent clinics. The renovated bungalow has ancient Tibetan baby carriers framed on the walls, rooms full of reproductive technology and a professional hum that belies the fact that life's big moments happen here every day. On any morning of the week, there are women coming in for egg pick-ups, scans, blood tests, donor sperm, ovulation monitoring and ovulation stimulation, and many have been coming for these treatments for years. On the morning I visited a number were pregnant.

Christine was 28 years old and had only been trying for a baby for six months when she went to her doctor suspecting something might be amiss. The GP referred her to the clinic. She had endometriosis and after surgical treatment for it, Christine went home and tried again for a pregnancy, without success. She had interuterine insemination (a process which sorts out the best sperm and delivers them to the egg at the right stage of its journey). She fell pregnant the first time but lost the baby at ten weeks. She had another three treatments of interuterine insemination and then went onto IVF. After producing 25 eggs, she had two put back and one took successfully. On the morning I saw her she had just passed 10 weeks gestation and she had been in and out of fertility treatment for four years—at a cost of $8000. This was the furthest she'd come along the track to having a baby, she was both excited and nervous and happy to talk even though her four-year trial has been a secret from most of her friends. 'No one knows I've had fertility problems,' she said. 'Going through IVF you shut everyone out, you don't talk to anyone. I suppose because I don't want to admit it. I'm a woman, I'm supposed to be able to have a baby. By the end, though, our marriage was really straining and I thought I was on my last chance.'

Simone, too, was shocked and angry when, at the age of 29, she discovered that her husband's sperm was 'hostile' to her eggs. 'I was really angry, I thought why did this happen to me, but I tried not to show it because my husband was pretty devastated.' Simone was also lucky. She fell pregnant on her first IVF treatment. When her son Jack was still a baby, she tried again but the second try took 18 months, until it produced a pregnancy and baby Sophie. Simone was now trying for a third. 'I kept thinking, do I want another? And every time I asked myself the question I thought, well, if I do, then I may as well do it now, when I'm 35, rather than wait. I just want to get it out of the way, because I don't want to spend any more time going through all these processes, all the thinking.' Indeed, by the time Simone either has another child or gives up on the idea, she will have spent seven to eight years of her life either in treatment or planning for it. She tried not to allow it to become too big a part of her life but the reality of fertility technology means she has made scores of trips in and out of the clinic with bulging ovaries and a hormone-rattled body; she's had scans of eggs and scans of her pregnancy; she's given blood, eggs and about $30 000. Her family was conceived here. As a midwife, she always had a realistic attitude to her fertility but she can't believe the attitude of others.

All these women I work with—there are about eight of them and some are in their late thirties—and they're still saying 'maybe I will, maybe I won't, maybe sooner, maybe later'. Some want to pay off the house and everything before they do it, another, she's 40, is adamant she's going to have a child, with or without a partner. I'm the youngest and they know what I've been through and they're still umming and ahhing.

Kerry, too, discovered problems early. At 26 she and her husband grew casual with contraception. Two years later they began investigating. At the clinic, they found her husband had a congenital problem that meant the sperm couldn't be ejaculated. After a batch of her husband's sperm was retrieved and IVF was tried, she fell pregnant and had a son, Connor. At age 32—still young by IVF measures—she has found the second child is proving more difficult. After a cost of about $10 000 and a number of cycles, none of the fertilised eggs have taken. When we spoke she had several eggs fertilised and many processes still to come. She says she always wanted three children, she is going for a second but she keeps telling herself she's lucky she had one. 'I hear people saying, one day I might have a baby and I say, don't wait, even if you're still in your twenties, you never know.'

Apart from biological age, there is another ticking bomb for this generation and that is sexually transmitted infections and, in particular, chlamydia. Often called the 'silent infection' because most are unaware they have it, chlamydia can cause infertility in both men and women, especially if it is left untreated. From 1991 to 2001, the incidence of chlamydia trebled in Australia and in just the one year from 2001 to 2002, notifications jumped from 20 200 to 24 000. According to Melbourne's Burnet Institute, most of the new cases are among 20- to 24-year-old heterosexuals and it's not necessarily among promiscuous people, just among those who have had multiple partners. Obviously, with young people spending more time unattached, their chances of getting the disease are greater. Marriage was once considered the best foil for STIs, just as education has proved the best form of contraception. But as more youth spend at least a decade moving between relationships, STIs have much more opportunity to spread.

All the work being done in reproductive fertility is uncovering more problems and, lately, the microscope has been focusing on problems with male fertility. More research is emerging on the male biological clock, which shows that even men in their thirties may start encountering problems. As men age, their sperm swim more slowly and instead of heading straight for the target, they begin to swim in circles (much like a man searching for the car keys). By the age of 50, men have a 67 per cent chance that their sperm are slow or meandering swimmers.

Like most modern men, that philosopher in Amanda Lohrey's book wasn't opposed to the idea of children, it was just a matter of timing. After all, his sister had two abortions so she could time the arrival of a child to fit into her long-service leave. All he argued about was deferring the decision to a more suitable time; he was, after all, a rational man. This fictional bloke was making the sort of rational decision that fills waiting rooms at clinics like Fertility First.

Having children is a choice and, according to Melbourne University philosopher Leslie Cannold, it's a choice we feel uncomfortable about. When she interviewed 35 childless women in Australia and America, Cannold found that most women were literally at a loss to explain why a woman should decide to become a mother. When she asked the women to name bad reasons for becoming a mother, half of them quickly offered eleven bad reasons. When she asked them to name good reasons, only three of them could find three good reasons. In interviews with these women, Cannold found that most felt that if they were going to take the fork in the road they needed good reasons to do it. When they couldn't come up with these good reasons, they concluded that mothering was an irrational act, probably something that was biologically inspired.[10]

Cannold and other philosophers argue that the rationalist orthodoxy that rules so much of our economic and political lives has infiltrated the way we think about all of life. When we come to think about having kids, we look for a reason and when we can't articulate a reason for kids, we wonder how valid such a decision is. We are better at talking ourselves out of the idea than talking ourselves into it.

The rationalist's approach to motherhood carries through to birth practices and the early months of a baby's life. Caesarean births in Australia occur in 22 per cent of all births. It's higher for private patients and higher for well-to-do women. Whether women are 'too posh to push', or more trusting in the knife than the midwife, or whether they simply want to schedule a birth day, obstetricians are under greater pressure to provide elective caesareans. Many women now approach the hospital gates knowing their conception date, their baby's gender, the bub's name and they have receipts for the booking at the childcare centre and the senior school. They may even arrive with an entourage of family and friends who will await the operation, with appropriately coloured flowers and name-embossed teddy bears. Surprise, it's a Grammar boy!

Some find pregnancy and birth such a shock, they never want to go there again. One of my school friends, who had one child, never wanted to see a birth centre again.

I would have considered having more children after my daughter if I could have found a surrogate and the whole egg harvesting thing was less invasive. The thought of going through another pregnancy was a major deterrent to enlarging the family.

American author Naomi Wolf called her book on motherhood, *Misconceptions*, largely because of the refrains she heard from women who'd had babies. Why wasn't I told? Why wasn't I prepared for this? I had no idea it would be like this. Why didn't someone tell me it would be so hard/scary/weird? Her book was partly an exploration of the world of pregnancy and childbirth she encountered when she became a mother. Although it probably wasn't her intent, much of the book reads like the journey of a powerful woman, used to controlling her own destiny, travelling through the world of biology, with all its unforeseeable troubles, humbling experiences and inevitable compromises.[11]

Women who come from small families and defer their own families grow more estranged from the messy process of having and raising children. As they grow more competent in the world of commerce, many find the adjustment to the other side more difficult. The sense of control and management women bring to the process of having babies makes many less able to cope with the unpredictable nature of babies, the intensity of feelings that motherhood brings or the unmanageable nature of a child who knows neither night or day, cries 24/7, feeds every half hour and doesn't even smile when you get it right.

Few people begin this process of having a baby with a good idea of what it's going to mean. When a baby is born, a mother and a father are born too. And they grow into their new roles in much the same way that a baby grows into a toddler and a primary school child grows into a beer-swilling teenager. The metamorphosis is as inexorable for the parents as it is for the child. Most of all, being a parent often changes you in ways that are completely unrelated to the economic, social, materialistic and rational world in which you made that decision to have a baby—with a mind full of mortgage calculations, paid leave, spare bedrooms and childcare costs. Of course, it changes everyone, but I suspect it has the biggest impact on women like me, the careerist, urban women who've made a home in the economic world. From the moment that pink stripe appears on the test strip, women like me enter the world of biology. And for many, it is a strange world full of emotions never encountered, passions never before ignited, challenges never faced. That pink stripe begins a personal journey into a future as parents but it also takes us into the history of humanity, it links us with our ancestors and creates a line into the future. How do you describe that world to

Lindsay, the philosopher, who scans the dark rooms of his Edwardian house planning one more renovation before tackling the question of children with his 36-year-old wife? Shifting the conversation about having children beyond dates, mortgages and Sunday sleep-ins is part of the challenge for a society that has constructed the era of rational choice; for the medical establishment, whose science has (almost) usurped biology; and for women, who have emerged on the other side of the pink stripe saying, 'Why didn't anyone tell me it would be like this?'

Ideology's orphan

3

In 1990 my daughter performed in a preschool play about the
environment. She was a washing machine and most of the boys
were chainsaws. Sitting in the audience on a grassy hill, I tried to
imagine how my daughter the washing machine fitted into the
destruction of the environment. The chainsaw dance was obvious—
old growth trees felled under the arms of three-year-old boys, native
birds fly off in fright, music becomes melancholic. But the
destructive power of washing machines was a more elusive concept,
one I vowed to ask the teachers about when I delivered my freshly
laundered child to them the following week. As Kate swirled around
the stage in a box stuck on spin cycle, I noticed that the baby's nappy
needed changing. I grabbed Toby, found a soft patch of grass and
then froze. He was wearing a disposable nappy. If I were to change
his disposable nappy that no doubt came from a 200-year-old Spotted
Gum in the Tasmanian wilderness, the audience would string me up
from the nearest Angophora. I took a deep breath and reminded
myself that I was a feminist before I was an environmentalist. If any

of those nice Green chaps wanted to help me wash my baby's nappies, I'd happily switch to cloth but I wasn't going to start cleaning up the world environment when I was so busy cleaning my own environment.

Feminism and environmentalism have been two major movements of the past few decades that have impacted on women's decisions to have children. Sometimes they have been bedmates, often they lived on different planets but each has served as a reference point for decisions about having children. Can I be a feminist and a mother? If I take a few years off work will I be letting myself down? Will I be letting the Cause down? Why do I feel as though I have stepped back into the 50s since I walked out of the maternity ward? Am I helping to destroy the planet by having a child? Is having a third child environmental vandalism? Do you get kicked out of Greenpeace for using Pampers? These niggling questions might not push women into a decision to have a child or not but they form the backdrop to discussions about children, on both a personal level and a social one. They form part of the landscape for those decisions in the same way that religion once informed decisions about children. Indeed, the values inculcated by women's independence and concern for the environment have largely supplanted the old religious imperatives surrounding family. At least, they have for many of the well-educated, urban women living in the developed world.

Religions once gave reasons for having children. It was God's plan, Allah's way or the right thing to do. It was written in the Bible and in the Koran. Religious ideologies have underpinned fertility for centuries. Its decline in societies and in the individual conscience has been accompanied by a decline in families across the world.

As religious influence waned so too did the pro-natalist push. In its place, many sought their values from more modern movements and some of those, especially feminism and environmentalism, were less convinced about the value of children in the modern world.

My first year out of school was the International Year of Women. In 1975, women were the stuff of headlines. The first Australian woman judge was sitting on the industrial bench, the first woman ambassador was at her post in Europe and the tabloids were regaling us with quirky stories about women down the mines, in zoos and in the cockpit (the headline writers loved punning on women in the cockpit). Hosties were becoming flight attendants, actresses were turning into actors, Ms was making its way onto government forms and chairmen were becoming just chairs (even taking the title of a piece of furniture was better than a sexist term). The language of equality was emerging, the statutes of equality were being formulated and the undergarments of oppression were being hoisted on burning flagpoles. Coming out into a world of possibility, my generation presumed a life of independence, equality, opportunity and a fair share of the drugs, sex and rock and roll.

With the blessing of the nuns, who had impressed on us the importance of a university education, my friends and I left school with our sights set on uni, the hippie trail (not so popular among the nuns) and a shared household. Unburdened by bras and the patriarchy, our talk revolved around which courses we would study, what jobs we wanted, when we'd travel and how many people we could fit into a shared terrace without the landlord freaking out. None of my friends talked about marriage and children. This probably isn't surprising among younger women now and it didn't seem odd at the time. But it was. I didn't realise how odd we were until I recently read Betty Friedan's *The Feminine Mystique*—one of the first books of the second wave of feminism published in 1963. Interviewing women in the late 50s and early 60s, Friedan says she was struck by a common theme among her generation. 'When we were growing up,' she wrote, 'many of us could not see ourselves beyond the age of twenty-one. We had no image of our own future, of ourselves as women.'[1] For Friedan's generation, there was no life beyond college except for marriage and motherhood.

Many of my generation had a blind spot too. It was marriage and children. Women like me didn't dream a future beyond our own self-development. For my friends, children belonged in a distant future and preferably someone else's future. At about the same time that school-leavers of 1975 were enjoying post-women's lib freedoms, the fertility rate dropped below replacement level for the first time ever and it kept dropping throughout the remainder of my generation's fertile years.

For some young women of the 70s and 80s that blind spot never cleared. They forged careers, lifestyles, relationships and identities in the spirit of the liberated woman and then turned around at the end of their fertile years and declared, I forgot to have children. Feminism, they said, had duped them. As journalist Virginia Haussegger wrote in the *Age* in July 2002, 'I am childless and I am angry. Angry that I was foolish to take the word of my feminist mothers as gospel. Angry that I was daft enough to believe female fulfilment came with a leather briefcase.'[2] Feminism, they said, had thrown out the baby with the bath water.

Did feminism let women down or were we afraid of letting feminism down?

Most of my friends discovered in time that they wanted to share their life with a partner and children, but it was a road less travelled in the 80s. The post-liberated mothers like me had to learn how to be a wife without being a doormat. My friends and I drew up our own marriage vows—editing out the obedience bit—and wore cream to show we didn't buy into that virginal white business. We figured out how to share household costs with a partner without surrendering financial independence. We divided domestic chores and tried not to be bitter when the division of labour failed. We had a baby and wondered why there were no pictures of dads in child-rearing books.

Looking back on the literature of women's liberation it's easy to conclude that if the women's movement of the early twentieth century lapsed after women had won the right to vote like men, then the women's revolution of the 70s gave up after winning the right to work like men. Both left unfinished business.

Is this too tough on feminism?

The impact of the women's liberation movement on my generation was in both policy fields and in our minds. It's pretty easy to follow the policy history. Less so our psyches. In researching for this chapter I came across one moment of enlightenment that helped me understand how feminism had shaped my attitudes without my knowing.

I have always hated the expression 'start a family' (even though I've probably used it in this book to avoid saying the word 'fertility' too often). To me, the expression 'starting a family' was archaic, it implied genealogy but there was something else about it too. It made me feel I was about to join a club that I wasn't sure I wanted to belong to. Perhaps it was because it was said by men so often—'Oh, so you're starting a family'—in a tone that was presumptive and paternalistic. Or maybe I didn't want this fantastically intimate experience of being pregnant to be placed within an institutional framework. I wasn't starting a family, I was having a baby. Reading the feminist literature of the 60s and 70s, I discovered where my loathing of the expression 'family' came from.

'Family' was the word that conservative forces used against women when men first started feeling threatened by the women's movement. 'But what about the family?' was the conservative catchcry. 'Is liberation destroying the family?', the headlines asked.

In her 1994 revision to her 1975 book, *Damned Whores and God's Police*, Anne Summers says she put the word 'family' in quotation marks to indicate she was referring to an ideological construct.[3] Kate Millet in her 1969 book, *Sexual Politics*, labelled the family as patriarchy's chief institution.[4] Germaine Greer in *The Female Eunuch* quotes Friedrich Engels' definition of the modern family in his book *The Origin of the Family*. The family, he wrote, is 'founded on the open or concealed slavery of the wife . . . Within the family, he is the bourgeois and his wife represents the proletariat'.[5] The post-war family had quotation marks around it like the suburban house had a picket fence around it. It had become a prison for women and an institution for men's privilege. It needed restructuring. And over the next two decades it would be deconstructed and rebuilt into loving groups of people in different relationships. But for some of us ingenues of the women's movement, the word 'family' never lost its sting and some of that misgiving leached into our future decisions.

Women's Liberation's attack on the 'family' was a turnaround from the rhetoric of the earlier movement. The suffragettes had always argued that they weren't out to destroy the family, and even Betty Friedan's ground-breaking *The Feminine Mystique* asked only for women to be able to combine their traditional roles in the house with work outside. Friedan conscientiously steered clear of the word 'career' lest people presume that she was advocating that women take their jobs more seriously than their home roles.

Even a very young woman today, must think of herself as a human being first, not as a mother with time on her hands, and make a life plan in terms of her own abilities, a commitment of her own to society with which her commitments as wife and mother can be integrated.[6]

Hardly revolutionary stuff. The fact that *The Feminine Mystique* had such an impact owes more to the time that it was published than to the radical nature of Friedan's message. When she was writing it, women were more captive to the home and hearth than they had been for decades. The divide between women who worked and those who became mothers was so sharp that she could write, 'I never knew a woman, when I was growing up, who used her mind, played her own part in the world and also loved and had children'.

But even as Friedan was writing the book, the pill was making its way into American homes—one million users in 1960, six million users by 1965. Once women had reliable control over the numbers of children they would have and when and if they would have them, their choices outside of that 50s stereotype began to open up. As the pill spread across the developed world, more women began going to university, more stayed to complete their education, the median age of marriage began to get older and the average age at which women had children got older. By the 1970s women were ready for a revolution.

And Women's Liberation was meant to be a revolution. Re-reading the literature from the late 60s and 70s, it's amazing to see how radical these ideas were and what a departure they were from the first wave of feminism. As Germaine Greer writes:

> In the old days ladies were anxious to point out that they did not seek to disrupt society or to unseat God. Marriage, the family, private property and the state were threatened by their actions but they were anxious to allay the fears of conservatives, and in doing so the suffragettes betrayed their own cause and prepared the way to the failure of emancipation.[7]

The women's movement of the early 70s wanted to overthrow not just all the patriarchal systems but traditional property rights, gender relationships and family structures. The movement was fuelled by the passions of the anti-Vietnam war movement, by the activism on campuses and by the sheer exuberance of that huge generation of baby boomers hitting adolescence and adulthood. Libertarianism, gay rights, censorship wars, sex, drugs and rock and roll—it was all up for grabs. Against that background, motherhood and the family was not the place to be.

Feminism's anti-family rhetoric is understandable for a couple of reasons. First, in the two decades leading up to the revolution women had been imprisoned in the role of wife and mother and activists knew that if women were to take a place in society they had to shed at least part, if not all, of their family persona. Not only was the family sucking up 24 hours of a woman's day, but the structure of the family dictated what sort of role a woman would have within the family and what role she could—or, more likely, couldn't—have outside the family. But beyond the banner beliefs of the movement was a more pernicious form of attack on motherhood. It was located more in the tone of women's literature than in the text. The subtext was suggesting that women's role as mothers was of no account, motherhood was second prize, the stuff that lesser women did, women of no education, no courage and no future. Motherhood was the Third World for modern women.

If there was vitriol behind much discussion of the family, then this too is understandable because women were finding that the family—their own family—was being used against them. In her history of Australian feminism, *Getting Equal*, Marilyn Lake recounts one of the early protests in 1965 when Ro Bognor and Merle Thornton (mother of actor Sigrid Thornton) chained themselves to a public bar after being refused a drink. The first question police asked Bognor when they came to unchain them was where her children were and who was looking after them. This was a refrain used against both the women's movement and against women themselves whenever they sought a larger role in society, whether it was the nineteenth-century suffragettes or the career women of the late twentieth century. Those words may well be the most personal form of attack in the political landscape. Little wonder that revolutionary women of the 70s decided they couldn't afford to wage a war if their babies were going to be used as weapons against them. War always causes a decline in fertility and these women were at war. As Lake wrote:

> Both in the threatened response of those who asked about the women's maternal responsibilities and in the women's seeming indifference to them, it became evident that it was the 'role' of mother that kept women in their place. Once lauded by feminists as valuable national work, worthy of political recognition and remuneration, motherhood had now come to be seen as the major barrier to women's freedom.[8]

But there was also an overriding social issue behind the anti-natalist push. The start of the 70s was the era of the population explosion. The high birth rate in the developed world in the 50s and 60s and the explosion in births in developing nations had culminated in the warning that the world was going to run out of food to feed the millions of extra mouths. The last thing the world needed, it seemed, was more babies. The women's movement was quick to align itself with the demographic imperative and with the emerging environmental movement. Greer wrote, 'The problem of the survival of humanity is not a matter of ensuring the birth of future generations but of limiting it'.[9] As the women's movement matured, it adopted some of the environmental concerns of the population explosion.

In her 1974 book, *The Future of Motherhood*, American Jessie Bernard says:

> It was not until the late 1960s that motherhood became a serious political issue in our country. Like so many other issues, it came not in clear-cut, carefully thought-through form but in a murky conglomerate of ecology, environmental protection and a 'welfare mess'. It took an anti-natalist slant. The problem posed was how to stop women from having so many babies.[10]

The irony is that at the height of the population panic women were already downsizing their dreams of babies. The peak year for the baby boom in most Western countries was in the early 60s, and by the 70s fertility in many developed countries had dropped below replacement levels. Women had got the message. There wasn't enough room in the world for their children, there wasn't enough time in the day for both children and work and there wasn't much of a future in having children.

After the 70s, much of the public momentum disappeared from the women's movement. It could be said that it split in two—the most radical were drawn into alternative movements and the more liberal feminists worked at making progress through government policy and workplaces. If the 80s were bereft of banners and pamphlets it might also have been because women were too busy making headway in the economic world. Between 1982 and 1989, women's participation in the workforce jumped from 45 per cent to 52 per cent, even after accounting for the fact that women were spending longer in education. The percentage of women in higher education grew so rapidly through the 80s that by the end of the decade there were more women—53 per cent—than men in tertiary education. The huge expansion of work in this period allowed women to enter the workplace at all levels. Part-time work rose from 16 per cent in 1980 to 20 per cent by the end of the decade and 28 per cent by the end of the century. Part-time work enabled women across society to combine work and motherhood, while the explosion in professional services opened the door for greater numbers of women in law, human resources, medicine, government, accounting and management. But perhaps women's success in moving into the workplace was just as much a function of the economy as of feminism. The huge growth in jobs, which demanded much more female participation than in the past, segued neatly into the demands of newly liberated women. Meeting the needs of mothers was on no one's agenda. The birth rate was just below replacement and whatever fall-off there was in individual birth rates was more than compensated for by the bulge of baby boomers having children, as well as record levels of immigration. Motherhood had become ancillary to the women's movement and inconvenient for the economy.

Through the 80s, childcare concerns occupied much of the movement's energies and, in this, they were very successful. When I had my first child in 1984, there were only two long-day childcare centres for babies within twenty kilometres of my home and only one nanny agency. By the time I had my third child in 1990, I could choose from half a dozen childcare centres within a few kilometres of home and there were three or four nanny agencies. During this decade, there were also groups agitating on behalf of mothers, focusing particularly on the biological load they carry with the birth of a child. Childbirth groups were lobbying for women to have a greater control in the birth process and breastfeeding groups, such as the Nursing Mothers' Association of Australia, were pushing for greater recognition of the importance of breastfeeding. But these groups were so culturally different to most feminist organisations that there was little communication between the two and little love lost.

In her 2001 book, *Our Bodies, Our Babies: The forgotten women's movement*, sociologist Kerreen Reiger says although 'the gap between mothers' organisations and organised feminism closed somewhat by the 1980s', the domain of motherhood was largely unexplored by feminism.[11] Some other books that questioned feminism's legacy were written by authors who'd spent their careers explaining birth, breastfeeding and how to make toys from corks and string.

In 1992, Sheila Kitzinger, queen of the natural birth movement, switched to a more political mode with the publication of her book, *Ourselves as Mothers*. 'Western culture,' she said, 'is anti-motherhood . . . Mothering (and fathering) has to be fitted into the cracks between all the important stuff of social life, such as politics, economics, commerce and industry. Becoming and being a mother is a second-rate activity.'[12]

So too, Penelope Leach, who guided many mothers of the 80s through 3 a.m. feeds and two-year-olds' tantrums, let loose with a volley against the anti-motherhood society in her 1994 book, *Children First*. She wrote:

> Wherever and whenever women's movements have begun, most of the personal, political and economic power has been in male hands so that the fastest escape routes from traditionally female roles has been traditionally male roles . . . Looking at the painful confusions that ignoring biologically based differences is creating for women and men when they come to produce the next generation, it seems that the route that ignores gender differences instead of honouring them may have

taken us closer to sexual equality but be incapable of taking us all the way.[13]

One Australian book that captured the feel of feminism in the 90s was the 1996 book, *DIY Feminism* edited by Kathy Bail. This collection of essays celebrated women who were making it by themselves, crafting their own identities through work, art, passions and lifestyles rather than through the prism of gender politics.[14] Reading through those stories it was easy to assume that feminism had done its job. And it had, for young women without children. Just one of those stories mentioned motherhood and her gritted-teeth account of life eloquently summed up modern motherhood.

By the end of the 90s, it was obvious that modern motherhood wasn't just a hot women's issue, it was *the* women's issue. As *DIY Feminism* had shown, women were enjoying liberation in many corners of their lives but once they undertook motherhood, the old barriers went up. It was clear that the workforce had accommodated women but the home was rife with gender inequities. The home still looked pretty much like the 50s bungalow. It hadn't been renovated by feminism, nor would it be renovated by capitalism. And there certainly wasn't a bloke around who was prepared to swing a hammer and take on the renovations. But the lies of modern motherhood were in the process of being exposed. Books, such as Susan Maushart's *The Mask of Motherhood* and Naomi Wolf's *Misconceptions*, would explore the silence and ambivalence of modern motherhood. These books gave titles to many of the feelings that women were encountering; they lifted the mask of superwoman and put a few pertinent questions on the political table. As Susan Maushart wrote:

Women can and do compete on a roughly equal footing with men in most of the arenas that legislation and social policy can touch. But there remain other places that they cannot touch, shadowy places in our minds and hearts and—perhaps most important of all—in our bellies. To put it bluntly, the feminist agenda has succeeded up to a point, and that point is motherhood.[15]

The ambivalence among women about what was expected of them in society and what they expected of themselves was touched upon by a few of my old school friends—the women who came out into the world in the International Year of Women. As a mother of two said:

My theory about why women are not having children these days seems clear. Basically, they are expected to have the children, bring up the children, be the 'ideal' of a perfect mother and have a successful career at the same time. The effort of trying to emulate the perfect mother is just too hard for today's women. Of course, the bleeding obvious is that motherhood is 'boring' and also hard work. I think I would have committed some crime if I had stayed in the traditional role and I sit here working hard on my farm with my two kids happy as Larry (whoever he is). In short, content but exhausted.

Another explained that she'd found joy in motherhood only after switching off her ideal of being superwoman and earth mother.

I am not an 'earth mother'—I hated breastfeeding, happily went to work to escape caring for anything under one year and doing domestic chores. Mind you, things changed for the third—I had a lovely time with two or three like-minded part-time working mothers on those days at home. We beached/coffee-ed and tea-ed often/exercised a bit and reminded each other to have sex with our husbands as often as possible.

By the start of the new century bookshops were turning their shelves of feminist literature over to self-help. A new genre of chick lit took up the task of chronicling the lives of modern women. And younger women were doing it themselves. To many of them equality was a given, not a movement. They would find their own way to be a woman at work and at home through their conversations around the water cooler, through email correspondence with work mates, through chick lit readings, television sit coms and negotiations with their partners. Younger women seemed to realise there was no template for being a modern woman, it was something that was still being sorted out, something that had a DIY stamp all over it. These younger women were, after all, products of the self-development movement, the self-made career path and the friends-as-family generation. They were used to making it happen for themselves. The language of equality and fairness was there but it was less likely to be couched in political rhetoric. But perhaps their older sisters, who had entered the adult world on a wave of feminism, didn't realise this. Many of them were still trying to live up to the expectations of a movement that had moved on. Maybe it wasn't so much a case of feminism letting them down but that they didn't want to let feminism down.

The new landscape of women's lives was finally canvassed in Anne Summers' 2003 book, *The End of Equality*. It asked why so many women at the start of the 21st century felt exhausted, trapped, discouraged and disheartened. Especially if they were mothers. Said Summers:

Despite the lip-service paid to motherhood, Australian society today demands a high price of women when they have babies. They are expected to give up so much. And young women today know that. It is not something most of them are going to do until they are really, really sure that it is the right thing—and the right time—for them.[16]

Fourteen years after Kate appeared in the preschool play as a washing machine, we were walking around a picturesque track in Sydney and I was explaining to her the implications of low birth rates on populations. I was, I suppose, subtly trying to imprint on her the idea that having kids is important. I'd just described how the population of Australia could shrink to five million in the next century if our fertility fell as low as Europe's levels and we gave up on immigration. 'Good,' she said, 'less people, better for the environment.' The dance of the washing machines was well learnt.

Since the early 80s, Australian children have been taught in school and through the media about the environment. Throughout those 25 years, children and youth have learned how Australians have spoilt their land through strip mining, intensive farming, suburban development, dirty factories, car use, sewage treatments, shopping bags that choke dolphins and cows that fart holes in the ozone layer. Environmental awareness came to the fore somewhat in 1989–90 when parents like myself installed five-way recycling systems in the kitchen, hid the baby's disposable nappies under fluffy pants and searched for dolphin-friendly cans of tuna in the supermarket.

The impact of this environmental education created a green movement that plays a crucial role in national politics today but it has also had a more insidious impact. Population growth has been so comprehensively linked with environmental degradation that many believe having children is environmental vandalism. In books such as *Child-Free Zone*, many of the couples say they chose to remain childless out of concern for the environment.[17] Whether that's a socially acceptable spin on their decision or a heartfelt one doesn't really matter but there is a widespread idea that choosing to have children is a blow to the environment. Youth comprise the greenest group in society largely because they've had a lifetime of learning about environmental degradation. But there was a subtext to the environmental message that many young people have accepted in theory, if not in their personal lives. The message is that humans have lost the privilege of replacing themselves because of the way they have treated the planet and that if young people really care about the environment, they won't add to the cause of the problem—humanity.

Paul Ehrlich was still warning the world of the environmental hazards of children in 1990. In a book published that year with his wife Anne, *The Population Explosion*, his emphasis had changed focus from the Third World population to the impact of First World babies on the future. 'Given the relatively enormous impact of the average baby in a rich nation on the resources and environment of Earth, the fewer there are, the better the children's chances will be to live in a habitable world.' Even as Europe was beginning to grapple with aging and decline, Ehrlich was still advocating one or two children, adding that 'if more Americans take the responsible step of having no children or only one, we could much sooner end growth'. How to achieve this downsizing of families? Ehrlich had a few tips. 'Talking casually about the population explosion with your friends will help . . . showing at least mild disapproval of irresponsible reproductive actions can also help to influence others. We, for example, don't give baby presents for any child past number two.'[18] The year that book was published, I had my third child. No wonder I didn't get much more than commiserations at his birth.

This environmental argument against children has worked on both the personal and the political level. On the personal level, it made it harder for youth to justify having a child, or even wanting children. For the most committed environmentalists, the only child a person in the developed world should have is one adopted from poorer nations. On a broader level, the environmental campaign against population relegated child-bearing to the realm of selfish indulgence. No longer could a woman have a child and think she might be bringing a scientist into the world or a poet or even a half-decent rap singer. No longer could she celebrate the birth of a new member of the family business or a visionary who would shape the world into a better place or someone who would make her laugh. Under the disapproving eyes of the environmentalist, she was delivering another mouth to feed, another set of footprints to despoil the earth, another consumer who would fill the natural world with the trash of modern life. This idea that parents were indulging themselves to the detriment of the planet further removed the family from political consideration. It was another reason not to support family—either politically, financially, commercially or philosophically. Environmentalism brought shame on motherhood—a shame that wasn't fair or justified.

Throughout the writing of this book, I found many people who welcomed the idea of lower birth rates because they believed that fewer people would be better for the health of the planet. As far as their own spaces are concerned, they believe that fewer people would be better for everyone. The morning traffic wouldn't be as bad; there would be less competition for housing so more people could afford them; there would be less competition for jobs; there'd be fewer people queuing to get into the supermarket. Urban life would be so much easier if a few of us would disappear! For the environment, the benefits of fewer footprints appear even greater. Many believe that if there weren't as many people then pollution would lessen, native forests would take over the salt-laden fields, suburbs would shrink, cities would become more sustainable, garbage would be manageable, dolphins wouldn't choke on plastic bags and all those starving Indians would be fed. If there was tolerance for those who had one or two children, it dropped away rapidly when people chose to have three or more children. This was especially the case when you arrived at a preschool play in a people mover with a plastic bag full of disposable nappies and a shallow understanding of how washing machines damaged the world waterways.

At a fundamental level, the debate about fertility is not a debate about population levels—at least not in Australia. Migration now provides most of Australia's annual population increase and it is migration levels that the government manipulates to reach economic or demographic goals.

As demographer Peter McDonald has pointed out, Australia's population is ramped up or down through immigration, not through natural increase. And if environmentalists want a stable and fairly low population then this is best achieved by having a relatively high fertility rate and low immigration. He writes:

> If fertility were to rise immediately to two children per woman and net migration was zero, Australia's population would reach zero growth at around 21 million people . . . However, if fertility fell to one child per woman and zero population growth was achieved through increased net migration, the population would eventually reach zero growth at around 35 million. Despite this well-publicised dynamic, many environmental scientists continue to celebrate the fall in fertility and one has even called for a one-child family for Australia.[19]

Many environmentalists and scientists do now recognise that environmental problems are management problems, not a matter of numbers. It is more important where we live on the continent and how we live than how many of us are on the continent. In his 2003 book, The Real Environmental Crisis, the American scientist, Jack Hollander, argues that it is poverty that is the environment's number one enemy, not population. 'My bottom line is that population growth per se should no longer be looked upon as a serious long-term global problem, environmental or otherwise. The real problem is poverty,' he says.[20] The environmental problems of poverty have traditionally been associated with developing countries and, in particular, the problem of not having enough money to deal with problems of rapid population increase. But poverty also arises in areas where populations are shrinking because they too lack the money and resources to manage the environment. As populations begin to shrink around the world this century, much of the environmental damage may well come from areas that no longer have the resources to maintain the environment.

In my Irish Catholic ancestry, there was a long held belief that a good Catholic woman was a pregnant one. Contraception was and still is banned by the Pope. Catholic women had a lot of children and if they had a child who became a priest or a nun, it bought kudos on the family: while the archetypal Jewish mother wanted her son to be a doctor, the iconic Catholic mother dreamed of her son joining the Jesuits. (One wonders whether the dearth of priests these days owes something to the downsizing of Catholic families.) In my poll of old school friends, only one had produced what could be called the classic large Catholic family (ten). Even though she only thought she'd have four children, she doesn't regret the somewhat larger family she ended up with.

Plenty of work, plenty of fun, sometimes hard to cope with getting everything done, but then everyone says that. Wouldn't be without any of them.

Her pithy response no doubt reflects a scarcity of time.

Up until the 70s, religion still played a large part in expanding world populations, both in the developed and the developing world. However, the decline of religious ideology has largely taken God out of the equation for many couples when they sit down to have their talk. Since 1971, the percentage of Australians who have a religious affiliation has dropped from 90 per cent to 73 per cent and even those who belong to a church have looser ties and more liberal ideas about the doctrine—they might be 'cultural Catholics' or 'lifestyle Buddhists'. In particular, the decline of big families in Australia has been associated with fewer people living strictly religious lives— especially among Catholics. But secularisation has also increasingly influenced the rise of smaller families.

· This influence can be seen in Australia at both ends of the demographic scale. Those who remain childless or have just one or two children are more likely to say they have no religion, those who have large families are more likely to have strong religious affiliations. A snapshot commissioned from the Australian Bureau of Statistics on the number of women aged 15 years and over who had ever had children shows strong religious ties with having children. Using the 1996 census, the survey shows that Jewish women are most likely to have children—71.5 per cent of adult Jewish women have had children. Just below them were women who identified themselves as Christian—71 per cent of them had had children. Muslim women were the third most fecund with 69 per cent of them having had children. Hindu women also were more likely to have children—68.5 per cent. The least number of children were born to women who had no religion. Only 57 per cent of women who had no religion had had children. Also low on the fertility stakes were Buddhist women, of whom only 59 per cent had children.

Large families might be disappearing off the secular map but they are still a feature across Christian, Muslim and Jewish communities. A working paper produced at the Australian National University in 2001 by Mohammad Jalal Abbasi-Shavazi and Gavin W. Jones showed that birth rates in Muslim countries were relatively high compared with more secular countries but they have been coming down in recent decades. In the early 80s, only four out of the world's 46 Muslim-dominated countries had birth rates of less than four per woman and many had rates of six children or higher. By the end of the century, half of the 46 countries had fertility of less than four and thirteen had birth rates of six or higher. When you look at the economic profiles of many of the Muslim countries, they are still very much developing countries—many are on the African sub-continent or in the Middle East. It seems obvious that as these countries develop economically, they are downsizing families in the same way that many Western countries have. Few would hazard a guess as to whether the sharp falls will continue at the same rate—and therefore fall into negative replacement territory eventually—or whether it will taper off at above replacement levels. Still, according to the research on current rates a quarter of the world's population will be Muslim by 2025.[21]

Throughout the centuries, different religious and ethnic groups have attempted to claim tomorrow through their wombs. It's not something that crops up in sermons too often but churches are increasingly worried by the baby strike. In August 2004, the Vatican released a document on men and women in the church, which took a surprisingly modern position on the role of women even though it expressed concern about low fertility. The *Letter to the Bishops of the*

Catholic Church on the Collaboration of Men and Women in the Church and in the World said in part:

> Although motherhood is a key element of women's identity, this does not mean women should be considered from the sole perspective of physical procreation. Women should be present in the world of work and in the organisation of society . . . women should have access to positions of responsibility which allow them to inspire the policies of nations and to promote innovative solutions to economic and social problems.[22]

Strangely, these words are reminiscent of what Betty Friedan was urging 40 years earlier.

Perhaps the Catholic Church had picked up on the message in demographic trends—child-bearing being abandoned in Catholic homelands such as Italy and Spain but continuing throughout the Islamic world. Fears about a Muslim-dominated world appeared in Phillip Longman's book, *The Empty Cradle*. Referring to the high birth rates in religious societies and the low rates in secular communities, he speculated that such a trend 'would drive human culture off its current market-driven, individualistic, modernist course and gradually create an antimarket culture dominated by fundamentalist values'.[23] It's worth noting that Longman is an economist based in Washington D.C. and a senior fellow at the New America Foundation. Nevertheless, both broad population trends and academic research support the idea that as people move away from traditional religions to less structured spiritual beliefs or no religious beliefs, they have fewer children. And, as societies move into more secular, market-orientated and individualistic philosophies, they have fewer children. Children are not just more common in poor countries but also in poor households (see Chapter 4).

The ideologies surrounding children's role in the world tend to seep into our consciousness, often without our realising it. It's a landscape of values that we don't notice until we sit down to draw it. Old ideas about the godliness of children might persist alongside new ideas about the destructiveness of populations on the landscape and the fundamental inequalities associated with having children that are so often experienced by women. Sometimes though, a simple idea can win the day.

I used to be a patient of a doctor who had pictures of both children and grandchildren on her wall. One day when I brought my two girls into her surgery—one for a bout of pneumonia that I'd missed—the doctor suggested to me that I have another child. It was out of the blue and I was stunned. No one had ever said to me that I should have another child. My environmental beliefs (flawed as they were) were telling me not to; my feminist background advised against it and I certainly wasn't going to do it for the church. I immediately thought—are my hips that big? But I had enough ego left to realise that the doctor was saying that I was doing okay as a mother and should bat on. It was the best compliment I've ever had.

Capitalism's child

A nnie, Sydney, mother of two, works in funds management:

As a young woman I swallowed the feminist mantra of having it all, hook, line and sinker . . . if I had a dollar for everyone that has said to me 'I don't know how you do it!' I would be a very rich woman. However, despite a very supportive spouse and a fabulous nanny, I recently decided that I didn't want to do it anymore . . . I don't want to be CEO anymore. Rather, I'll settle for a part-time job that gives me some professional satisfaction. Having experienced the feminist ideal of being superwoman, my definition of 'having it all' has changed dramatically.

Hazel, Sydney:

As a mother of three children (11, 14 and 16) I have been juggling full-time work and home life for sixteen years. I was conned! I am exhausted. I have spent my work life pretending that I didn't have a family and my home life has become a strategic exercise in trying to fit everything in each day . . . I have found that children take more, not less of your time as they get older. I have now decided to work part-time. I doubt that my work colleagues will understand.

These emails arrived in the ABC online chatroom on 23 February 2004, after a discussion on Sally Loane's Morning program on Sydney radio. That day there were scores of responses to the 'BBQ stopper' issue of managing work and life. The stories were personal and had such heat in them, it was as if they'd bubbled up from a deep well of frustration, resentment and struggle. They scorched the screen. By 2004, work–life balance had become an issue for both sides of politics—for Prime Minister John Howard, who was trying to renovate his white-picket-fence view of family, and for Opposition leader Mark Latham, who was barnstorming the schools of Australia with a children's book in his hand. But even as the genie of modern family life was escaping from its bottle, there were moves to put the stopper back in. The heat in this debate was such that politicians kept switching back to safer territory like terrorism, economics and tax. Anything seemed easier than that emotional landscape of the family. Just scrolling through the listeners' responses that morning unearthed wrecked lives, derailed careers, lonely children, callous companies, emotional eunuchs and stressed marriages. And every one of those personal cries was political.

If women's liberation skirted around the motherhood issue and environmentalism undermined it, then capitalism poleaxed it. During the 90s, the turbo-charged capitalism that accompanied the era of economic liberalism reshaped working lives. For most people the change occurred in a vice-like way—a turn of the screw put more pressure on hours; another turn squeezed incomes; another turn gave a promotion and a longer shift at the office; another pushed out security; a finer adjustment quashed debate in the workplace. The pressure on workers was relentless and by 2003–04, you only had to put a microphone in front of the average person to hear the screams of a stressed society. And, like tortured mice in a cage, a stressed society doesn't reproduce itself.

The impact of the market-dictated society was most obvious in work lives. The market's annexation of intimate lives pushed people deeper and longer into the workplace—the average worker literally spent more hours every day working. As other parts of life shrivelled, identities could be summed up by what was written on business cards, or on the shingle outside the office or on the back of the ute. The march of the market left little space or time for the domestic sphere—homes emptied, streets grew quiet and social life took a dive. We told each other that we'd 'catch up', 'do lunch' or 'get together soon' but we never did. The 'other' part of life became contingent on priorities at work. The marketplace invaded in more insidious ways too. It commercialised relationships—the middle class paid for child care, outsourced housework, sought security in window grilles rather than neighbours and raised children with tutors, extra-curricular lessons and holiday camps. It infiltrated the language and therefore the way we thought about the world. We held people to account; we sought closure from events; we looked at the bottom line of everything and we did our sums on having children. And finally the individualisation of the market economy stole the collective voice—the voice that had once been expressed in feminism, unions, religions, clubs or community. We're now DIY feminists, we're independent contractors, we're self-helpers, we're bowling alone, we're home alone and we're on our own.

Eileen, Corrimal, 42-year-old single mother of two:

What many employers seem to want is a workforce of 'nuns' and 'monks'; employees who are 100 per cent devoted to the workplace, forsaking family, friends, relationships and pleasure. In my workplace, it seems that the only ones rising through the ranks are either single and married to the job or who leave the child-rearing to an at-home spouse, grandparents or paid child carers.

In 1907, the Harvester judgment established in Australia a needs-based basic wage that recognised that a worker needed to support his wife and three or four children. Work was cast around the reality of families (and the male-centred view of work). As Eileen from Corrimal wrote in the ABC chatroom, times have changed. Almost a century later, employers prefer to pretend that a worker has no obligations outside the workplace, no devotions greater than the full-time job.

The career woman is where the popular concept of childlessness resides. She is the modern incarnation of the women's libber, she rode the boom in education in the 70s and 80s and then rode the expansion in the workforce during the 80s and 90s. She can work like a man but in her relationships she pays a price that few men must pay. By her early forties, the well-educated, single woman will go to a bar and find there are three single women like her for every two unmarried men of her class. And, if she lives in a capital city, she'll find even fewer single men because of the geographical work pressures that leave men on the land but lure women to the city. Those high-achieving women who do have a partner are less likely to have a child. According to the 1996 census, women who haven't had any education outside of school will have had 2.3 children by the time they're 40 years old, those with a degree will have had 1.8 children and those with higher degrees just 1.3 children. Higher education is still the most effective form of contraception for the modern woman. Only 11 per cent of women who don't have tertiary education end up childless; yet twice as many (22 per cent) women with degrees will not have any children and more than a third (34 per cent) of women with higher degrees will never have a child. The higher up the career ladder, the more empty cradles. For working women's spear-carriers, the cost of extended education and of working in a men's culture has been in their relationships. Both women and men working full-time are working longer hours—up from 38.2 hours a week in 1982 to 41.3 hours in 2001—and they're working more intensely than ever. Productivity changes that downsize companies leave survivors with bigger workloads; cultural changes in companies have eroded lunch breaks, opened up offices earlier and extended the day so far into the night that many feel like time thieves if they leave before 7.30 p.m. They may have six-figure salaries and *Sex and the City* lifestyles but the demands of the workplace have turned high-achieving women into modern versions of those monks and nuns who retreated to medieval cloisters to devote their lives to God.

High-income couples have the most to lose when they broach the subject of having children. And the person who elects to be the main caregiver, usually the woman, faces a double jeopardy. In the period away from work, or in diminished work obligations, a woman not only loses a large income but also finds herself dependent on her partner for probably the first time in her life. Often, the old gender patterns of household finance emerge and the independent career woman finds herself asking for hand-outs or explaining expenditures. At work, she becomes a second-class citizen. She has inconvenienced her employer and when she returns she is expected to give the same 24/7 commitment. Moreover, her period outside of the workforce and any subsequent diminution in her working patterns will erode her superannuation and she may find herself forever after on the hand-outs end of family finances.

Companies now boast 'family-friendly policies'. But in many large companies, these polices are little more than 'cover stories', because if the culture within the companies revolves around the heroic, marathon worker who will sleep on the office floor to get a deal done, then other sorts of workers are, by default, losers. Workers leave the coalface of the corporate culture at their peril. Fathers are especially reluctant to leave the realm of the super worker to take advantage of parental leave allowances or flexible working arrangements. Around the world, the introduction of paternity leave has been greeted by indifference, especially in the first few years of its introduction. Whether this reflects fear of losing points at work, or fear of dirty nappies at home, or both, has been teased out in a few studies.

Psychologist Graeme Russell at Macquarie University has explored attitudes of fathers as part of the Fatherhood audit for the federal government. While fathers usually blame work demands for impacting on their ability to be active fathers, Russell has found that many men have more control over their working hours than they like to admit. He also found that the reasons men don't take advantage of family-friendly policies are more complex than they like to admit. The fact that many fathers choose to prioritise work has more to do with how they view themselves as workers and how they view their partner's role and, indeed, whether their partners really do want their presence at home.[1]

Fathers who retreat further into the workplace when babies are born never learn to be competent around babies. The physics of nappies can defeat a Nobel-prize winning scientist; a bout of colic can undo a marathon runner and a man from McKinseys can be bamboozled by a simple feeding schedule. Even the act of playing peek-a-boo with his bub may feel foreign to the over-worked dad. Over-worked fathers don't just miss out on bedtime stories, they are often moody and unresponsive when they come home, so the quality of the time with their kids suffers. Often the too-busy father remains too busy for most of the child's life and, therefore, a stranger to the intimate bonds of paternity. The era of over-work pushes fathers back to that 50s stereotype of the aloof father, a daily visitor to the home.

Michelle, Sydney, two young children:

Prior to children, I had a career, post-children I had nothing. I felt as though I was punished for having children. I had a job and now I had nothing with very little prospect of finding part-time work in my profession. In my discussions with my former boss, a female in her mid-30s with no children, I expressed my disappointment and hoped that, for the sake of all our futures, a representative sample of Australians reproduced in the future . . . her advice was to find a 'family friendly' company to work for!

That online correspondent had either intuitively or knowingly tapped into one of the biggest hypocrisies of the corporate world's treatment of parents. It is not mothers who are coasting on corporate generosity; it is companies that are riding on the backs of mothers. This was one of the conclusions that Michael Bittman and Jocelyn Pixley made in their 1997 book, *The Double Life of the Family*[2] (see Chapter 7).

The same point is made in the 2002 fictional book, *I Don't Know How She Does It*, by London writer and mother of two, Allison Pearson. The story of Kate Reddy, a successful funds manager and mother of two, took Pearson onto bestseller lists around the world and into the hearts of working mothers everywhere, because so much of Kate

Reddy's story was their story. At the funeral of a girlfriend, Kate Reddy recalls her friend's struggle to balance work and family. Then she remembers something her friend told her:

> 'The thing is, Kate,' Jill said, 'they treat us as though they're doing us a great favour by letting us go back to work after we've had a child. And the price we pay for that favour is not making a fuss, not letting on how life can never be the same for us again. But always remember it's we who are doing them the favour. We're perpetuating the human race and there's nothing more important than that. Where are they going to get their bloody clients from if we stop breeding?'[3]

Rhonda, Northern Beaches:

I'm a single 33-year-old running my own business. I work 70–80 hours a week and literally have NO TIME to even LOOK for a partner, let alone put the time into sustaining a relationship.

While the childless career woman is the icon of the fertility debate, it's those women struggling to raise children and hold down a full-time job who are the most stressed in both their child-rearing and their work. These are the archetypal women who check their lapels for vomit as they walk into the office; who leave an old jacket over the back of their chairs after they sneak out at 5.30 p.m. and who whisper cooking instructions into mobile phones during meetings. These women are working in jobs that were designed for men with a wife at home and yet they are trying to mother in the same way as the full-time mother does.

Adelaide academic, Barbara Pocock, interviewed hundreds of women for her 2003 book, The Work/Life Collision, and found that while our personal lives have undergone a revolution, the workplace still operates around archaic ideas. Changes in work practices, she said,

> are not mirrored in compensating changes in key cultures and institutions that shape behaviours at work, at home and in the market. Australian households reveal not only unchanging patterns of domestic and care work that remain largely the work of women but also of unrenovated models of motherhood and fatherhood, and workplaces that still have at their centre an 'ideal-worker' who is care-less.4

I Don't Know How She Does It is crammed with graphic accounts of the juggled life. At one stage, Kate Reddy is watching the television program ER and she realises that her life is like the triage job of the nurse in the emergency room.

> Daily existence was a constant assessment of who needed my attention most: the children, the office or my husband. You'll notice I leave myself out of that list and that's not because I'm a good and selfless person. Far from it. Selfishness just wasn't an option; no time . . . When I wasn't at work, I had to be a mother; when I wasn't being a mother, I owed it to work to be at work. Time off for myself felt like stealing. The fact that no man I knew ever felt that way didn't help.5

To buy into the male world of work, women find they have to pretend that their other life doesn't exist. They have to make like men who have wives at home. I remember the horror of fielding work calls at home after 6 p.m. A home at 6 p.m. with three young children isn't the ideal space to conduct a professional meeting. It would be hard to think of a worse one. As they agitated around the phone I'd feed the children biscuits much like an animal trainer feeding fish to seals. Sometimes, I'd stretch the phone to the bathroom and hope the children wouldn't need to use the toilet. If the children made a ruckus, one particular editor would ask, 'Do you want to do something about that?' I suppose she thought she was being considerate, giving me permission to fix up the problem. But when she said it, I thought, 'What do you want me to do? Turn down their volume? Gag them with a nappy?' In retrospect, I should have asked callers to ring me during work hours but that would have been a black mark against my commitment and mothers can't afford too many of those.

A cruel irony of the intensification of work during the past two decades is that those workers who have the most demands placed upon them are those who are at the peak age for having children. Employers have a preference for those aged 25 to 40 years—that's the age when they're ambitious enough and energetic enough to work the 24/7 shifts. They are also the years when the majority of people will have small children so, in that decade, they must be peak performers at both work and home. Ten years earlier, they wouldn't be so progressed in careers so home life might be more manageable; ten years later they might be shifting into less intense forms of work. But neither the corporate world, nor biology cut them much slack.

Mothers in the two-career household tend to compensate by either having fewer children or downshifting into less demanding work. Many find the experience of juggling their first child with work so difficult, the first child becomes their last. There is anecdotal evidence that it is the most career-minded women who end up with just one child. Certainly, the number of one-child families is growing. In the 1996 census, a snapshot of the number of families with children (under 15) showed that one-child families just outnumbered two-child families. One-child families stood at 1.15 million and two-child families trailed by 10 000 at 1.14 million. Just one census later, in 2001, one-child families outnumbered two-child ones by more than 100 000—that is, there were 958 000 one-child families and 839 000 with two children. In one night's snapshot of families, 70 per cent have no children under the age of fifteen living with them, 13 per cent have one child, 11 per cent have two children, 4 per cent have three children and only 1 per cent have that family so revered in the 50s—four children. Some of those families with one child will go on to have another one and some have other grown-up children but, at any one time in Australian society, there are many more only children than there are children with siblings. The increase in the number of families who have one child occurred during that period when work both intensified in nature and extended in hours.

The other route working mothers take is to reduce their work commitments. Many surveys show that once women reach a certain level of their career and a certain age, they jump off the career ladder. Some form their own businesses—they are both more likely to start small businesses and more successful in them—some take the mommy track or a more limited career track. But the effect is the same—a generation after women's liberation, women are once again having to choose between career and family.

Kim, 31, two small children, now working from home:

I've realised that a career is actually shorthand for meaningful and enjoyable work, not how many hours you put in at an office (I would dare say I am more productive in the four hours I do at home than the eight or more I was spending in the office) or how big the pay packet is. I guess I'm glad I've learnt this lesson at 31, not 41 or 51 when my children have grown up knowing no different to Mum being permanently cranky and tired and never home.

The most common profile for working families is one full-time wage-earner and another in part-time work, mostly the mother. Australians are lucky, in one sense, that the country has one of the highest levels of part-time work in the developed world. Much of this part-time work was created in those two decades the 80s and the 90s, when women's participation rate in the workforce rocketed. In those two decades, part-time work doubled from 15 per cent of the total workforce to 28 per cent and most of the part-timers are women. Almost half the women in the workforce (46 per cent) work part-time, compared with only 15 per cent of men. Most women who work part-time seem happy with their hours but this often has more to do with the fact that it suits their family life rather than their satisfaction with the job.

In the 2001 HILDA survey which is conducted regularly for the federal government's Department of Family and Community Services only a quarter of women working part-time say that they miss out on family activities because of work commitments. The same study, however, found that half of full-time working women say they're missing out.[6] But part-time workers pay dearly for the privilege of taking the time to watch children at sporting carnivals or pick them up after school. Says Pocock in *Work/Life Collision*:

> *Many workers find that part-time work meets their needs, they want to be available for their families and avoid the stress of full-time jobs. They also understand the costs of working part-time: for job security, a career and higher earnings. Many—even those in permanent, secure part-time jobs—accept that they have 'a job not a career'. They see this 'choice' as between greedy, demanding full-time, career jobs and being the peripheral part-timer.[7]*

These fears of being pushed to the periphery of the workforce are well founded. As the authors of the 2004 book *Better Than Sex* say, HR departments shudder every time someone comes in asking for part-time work.

Despite paying lip service to company policies on work/life balance, informally they worry it may set an unhealthy precedent, it's disrupting for the flow of work, or others will be resentful. Part-time work is disparaged by many employees and managers alike.[8]

Helen Trinca and Catherine Fox should know. They report on management issues for the *Australian Financial Review* and know the difference between company policy and company practice.

Perhaps the most barren area for family life is down at the bottom of the career ladder. The working poor have borne the brunt of tough economics, both at work and at home. The blue-collar worker was the soul of the union movement and, largely through union efforts, these workers could once earn a family wage while working reasonable hours in secure jobs. In the past few decades, the blue-collar workforce has been decimated. Now, most unskilled people work in casual jobs, with insecurity, low pay and haphazard shifts.

According to the Australian Centre for Industrial Research and Training, almost 90 per cent of the new jobs created during the 90s paid less than $26 000 a year. Nearly half of the new jobs paid less than $15 600. For unskilled men, work is insecure and low-paid and this makes their family life insecure and lonely. A study done for the Australian Family Association in 2004 by the Monash University Centre for Population and Urban Research called 'Men and Women Apart', shows that these men aren't finding partners. Only 50 per cent of men who earn under $16 000 a year have partners and only 65 per cent of men who earn under $31 000 have found partners. This compares with the 80 per cent of men earning $78 000-plus who have partners. Moreover, the low-paid men are at least twice as likely as high-income earners to be divorced.9 For many men, a steady wage and a home are the prerequisites for marriage and family. They see a good job as something they must take into a marriage and, much of the time, their potential partners see it as necessary. For many men today, the steady home life will be as hard to find as the steady job. The impact on birth rates for the working poor man is hard to gauge, if only because fertility is a measure of how many children women have, not men. Certainly, some of these unpartnered men would have fathered children with some of the single mothers, who also dominate the lower socio-economic ranks, but many will never know fatherhood.

At the bottom of the economic pile are those families where neither parent works. According to the Australian Bureau of Statistics figures, in 2001 there were 350 000 families where neither parent was employed. This pool of unemployed parents was so big that almost one in five children (under the age of fifteen) lived in households where neither parent worked. These are overwhelmingly poor families—80 per cent have an income of less than $300 a week—they are outside of the work/spend cycle and more isolated socially than employed families. They do, however, have more children. More than a quarter of them has three or more children. So, while women at the top of the socio-economic pile are having few children, women at the bottom are having more than average. One way or another, children are increasingly becoming associated with underprivilege.

Annie, Sydney:

I met a young woman in a business I visited (I was a consultant and took my own three-month-old child along to the meeting).

This young woman admired my son and said she also had a young baby. I asked her if she missed him and she told me that she didn't really. She also said that she was lucky that she had to go back to work when he was only six weeks old as it meant that she did not get attached to him.

Most of the discussion of the work–life balance centres on the working side of the equation. It is, after all, the nature of work that has changed so radically; and people can count the extra hours spent at work; they can see the results of work in pay packets, in CVs and in the heels of their shoes. But work casts a shadow on domestic lives and, as work assumes a greater presence in most people's lives, the world outside contracts into a dark corner. Eight hours work, eight hours play, eight hours sleep—150 years ago it seemed a reasonable request. But what was fair for the stonemasons of nineteenth-century Australia isn't attainable for families of the 21st.

The issue of housework is the other side of women's working lives. It is something of an invisible double shift because it's hidden in the domestic space, not conducted in the public space like paid work. Housework is one of the unrenovated areas of women's lives and it's a double burden that erodes relationships, hampers women's commitment to the paid workforce and literally shrinks families. The impact of unequal domestic duties on birth rates hasn't been studied much, if only because it is such a slippery concept trying to figure out who does what around the nation's sinks. Most couples can't agree on who does the daily domestics in their home, much less what goes on into the Gross Domestic Product. Still, there is preliminary work from Brown University in the United States by Joost de Laat and Almudena Sevilla-Sanz that links unequal housework to low birth rates. The average working woman in low-fertility Italy still does 88 per cent of the housework, and in Spain—another very low fertility country—women do 83 per cent of the domestic work. In northern European countries, where birth rates are higher, women do between 64 and 67 per cent of the housework.[10]

The erosion of private lives, the squeeze on leisure and the contraction of domestic spheres aren't just lifestyle issues. The home is where the family resides and, in particular, it's where children are traditionally raised. And I say 'traditionally' because the family has largely moved out of the home. With most parents in the workforce and many working long hours, parents are home for fewer hours of the day. Children too are increasingly strangers to the home as they spend more time in childcare centres, schools, after-school activities and even boarding schools. And with no one at home to hold the fort, increasingly, domestic chores are being outsourced or they consume the weekend.

The well-to-do are becoming strangers in their own home and the poorer are becoming serfs in their own home.

The biggest growth industries in the past two decades have been in servicing households. The first service for a family that's pressured for time is cleaning. After the cleaners come lawn carers and gardeners. Next, the cooking is outsourced to takeaway providers or it's replaced by a last-minute dash to the supermarket for semi-prepared meals. The service industry thrives on the stress of households. Indeed, when you examine traffic patterns in major cities, you find that there has been a huge increase in cars coming into middle-class and wealthy suburbs during the day. The homes may be empty but they are being serviced during the day in the same way that offices are serviced at night.

Those with enough income have turned many private parts of their lives over to commerce. And that means they're amateurs at domestic life. They may love the fact that they never have to clean a toilet bowl, but that privilege makes them less competent in the space that has traditionally been reserved for children and family. Working parents who can't afford home services find themselves spending much of their reduced leisure hours on household chores. In these homes, neither the father nor the mother can feel a sense of refuge or relaxation, they are both serfs in the domestic sphere.

Work sometimes feels like home and home feels like work. This was the sub-heading of a 1997 book, *The Time Bind: When work becomes home and home becomes work*, by American sociologist Arlie Hochschild. After spending three years interviewing all levels of workers at a large American company, Hochschild found what generations of men have long known: work is an escape from the pressures of home. As she investigated company policies on work–life balance, she discovered that many times the policies didn't work because the employees didn't want to use them. Employees, she said, were 'responding to a powerful process that is devaluing . . . the essence of family life'.[11]

The hollowing out of our homes is partly a product of the loneliness of suburbia but it's also due to the greater appeal of workplaces. Despite the trend to over-work, many people find that their workplaces are pleasant, stimulating and rewarding. They are often places where people feel most competent, most in control, and this is especially highlighted for parents who often feel incompetent and out of control in the home. As Barbara Pocock found when she interviewed working mothers: 'Many see the workplace as a place where they have laughs, fun and social life: as one put it "Your work becomes your network".'[12]

At the end of the twentieth century, the workplace was undergoing a revolution. High-tech ventures were cropping up around cities in the middle of the technology boom. The nerds of IT brought with them new economy offices, with playrooms, free vending machines and dress-down codes. This more relaxed way of working began infiltrating mainstream offices.

The monthly magazine produced by the Australian Human Resources Institute often runs lists of lifestyle benefits that companies offer. In the June 2004 issue, the magazine listed more than twenty major companies that offer such services as yoga, massage, walking groups, gyms, medical checks, subsidised cafes, meditation, stress management workshops, tennis coaching, private health insurance and sailing competitions.[13] One Sydney law firm offers its lawyers a range of services to keep them at their desks late into the evening. They have free massages, meal delivery service to their desks, taxi cards to pay their way around town, free espresso services, unlimited use of phones and Internet for personal purposes and, at a pinch, a concierge service that will pick up their dry-cleaning, book holidays and buy a birthday present for the spouse. Of course, this is all aimed at keeping the lawyers working late but it's little wonder that these lawyers don't want to go home, where they so often feel like interlopers.

In *Better than Sex*, the authors explore in great depth how work has annexed our private lives—often with our approval. The book, they wrote, was an attempt to look 'beyond the slog to see why it is that we allow work to be so powerful. We want to understand why people feel like winners, not losers, when they spend long hours in the office, why they put work ahead of family, religion and leisure and make it the main measure of human value.'[14] And they discovered why. The organisations of the modern era are no longer content to have our labour for defined parts of the day; they want all of our energies, our creativity and our passions. They want us to be part of their mission. They want it 24/7. And they'll reward it when it's given.

The bottom line is that we are supported at work. We have assistants, managers, food on tap, a quiet environment, like-minded company and no one vomits on your lapel after lunch. At work someone else cleans, someone else maintains the systems, someone gives us money for our time and no one wants us to take the garbage out at the end of the day. At home, there are no supports—we have to manage the household, arbitrate over who does what, arrange for the washer to be fixed, bring food into the kitchen and someone has to do something about the rubbish under the lounge cushions! For all this we pay dearly, either in dollars, our time or our tempers. In many ways, at work we all have 'wives', but at home very few have 'wives'.

These fundamental forces are reshaping our lives in ways that are often not fully appreciated. This is reflected in the tendency to work late when children are young (a particular trait of the male careerist); in the difficulty of managing the mental transition from work mode to home mode; in the sense of being a stranger in your own home (who put that there?); and the realisation that you might know what your company's budget is next year but you have no idea when the nine-year-old last did his homework, brushed his teeth or, indeed, whether he is still nine years old.

This divorce from domesticity caught Kate Reddy (in *I Don't Know How She Does It*) by surprise on Christmas Day. She was reflecting on how different she was from the women's 'muffia' who kept home and hearth, treated men like livestock that needed husbandry and cooked mince pies on time (and without help from the Woolies freezer section).

I expect a man—my man—to do women's work because if he doesn't I can't do a man's work. And up here in Yorkshire the pride that I feel in managing, the fact that I can and do make our lives stay on track,

if only just, curdles into unease. Suddenly I realised that a family needs
a lot of care, a lubricant to keep it running smoothly; whereas my little
family is just about bumping along and the brakes are starting to
squeal.[15]

The estrangement from intimacy and the commercialisation of relationships was explored in a series of essays by Arlie Hochschild in her more recent book, *The Commercialisation of Intimate Life.*[16] She chronicled how many of the negotiations we make every day with family and friends and workmates are increasingly shaped by capitalism. These sorts of negotiations are making incursions into relationships between parents and children. They're reflected in the concept of 'quality time' and the idea that all meaningful interactions with children can be timetabled and condensed. It's also obvious in the language of child development. Instead of watching children grow, parents monitor development, check scores and get reports on their progress from child carers, teachers, nannies and grandparents. Parents on the work treadmill are less able to tune into the ebbs and flows of children's moods, so find themselves running crisis control systems and just-in-time emotional responses. Sometimes it seems easier to do what the friend of that ABC listener did—don't bother getting attached to our children because then it's easy to get back to work. Back to normal. Back to what our employers want. We can become what Naomi Wolf in *Misconceptions* called 'machine mom'.

This is the ideal of the superfunctional mother/worker, who is able to
work at top capacity up to the due date, takes one to three months off
to deliver, nurture and bond, finds top-notch child-care, and returns to
work, where, if she breastfeeds, she will pump discreetly in the employee
ladies' room.[17]

The managerialism in our homes also turns couples into tag-teams—passing on children, responsibilities and commitments like a baton in a relay. Communication degenerates into a series of night-time thumps on the back when the baby cries or instructions passed by phone message, email or through gritted teeth. And when the fights become too much, the market is called upon to sort it out—get a cleaner, get takeaway, put the kid into preschool care!

As Penelope Leach says in *Children First*:

> There is a broader, vaguer unease that many parents share but most rarely voice: a sense of loss, even foreboding, arising from leaving much of their children's socialisation, education and acculturation to paid labour and the values of the marketplace. Post-industrial societies increasingly consider it normal for the children [who] parents have for love to spend most of their waking hours with people whose job is to care for them for money.[18]

We have become a society of homo economicus—creatures who have evolved into economic beings. The challenges of family life become just another set of equations to be weighed rationally, managed sensibly and expedited efficiently. The joy of children has always been partly an escape from the adult world into the land of awe, spontaneity, silliness, magic and carelessness. But homo economicus don't have time to go there, or maybe they're just so imbued with the rational world that they don't see the magic any more.

Work that consumes the bulk of the day's time and energy doesn't leave time enough to have children, raise children, enjoy children or even want them in the first place. And a working culture that has hollowed out home life doesn't create an environment conducive to spending time with children or for moulding a family life. When the office becomes sanctuary and home becomes a chore, there's something weird happening in the world.

Fiona, 37, two young children:

I definitely see this as a society issue—not just about mothers. The more we accept that long hours are the only way to work, the more we diminish the value of family and community connections.

Home 5 alone

My elder daughter is attending first-year university. She lives at home, works at a part-time job to support her habits and likes the university life so much she's thinking of staying on for a long time. A long, long time. I try not to be judgmental. I try not to point out that when I was her age, I'd moved out of home, bought my own car, dropped out of uni, begun my life-long career and established an independent life, a credit rating and a few bad habits. Sometimes, I crack. 'When I was your age, I was . . . blah, blah, blah.' She's tolerant. She reminds me that these are different times; that the world needs more educated workers, fewer home buyers and women who can shimmy into a fashionable bar without paying a cover charge or paying for it later. And she's right.

We live in exciting times. Relationships are more fluid than ever and more flighty. They mean different things at different times and they are built around our desires, rather than society's definition of what they're meant to be. The varieties of intimate relationships are such that the Alternatives to Marriage Project lists 40 different terms on its website to describe couples who aren't married, ranging from 'spousal equivalent' and 'collaborative couple' to 'sweetie'.

Women once spent most of their lives as daughters then as wives and mothers, but today's women might shift between being single, a hook-up, a de facto, an ex, a sometime girlfriend, a virtual girlfriend, a wife, mother, step-mother, divorcee, second-time bride and quite possibly a multiple divorcee. Men once graduated from son to dad and breadwinner, but the man of today bounces between hook-ups, pick-ups, platonic relationships with women, de facto arrangements, possibly a fling with a bloke, and marriage and divorce. And he probably won't be sole breadwinner in any of those roles. Even in steady relationships, people's definitions of that relationship may change. I find myself switching descriptions all the time. Sometimes, I'll say I'm a 'wife' and sometimes a 'partner', depending on my mood and what point I want to make. I must admit, most of the time I'd prefer to be called a girlfriend as that doesn't usually entail washing obligations or a duty to remember where the car keys are.

But the mercurial nature of relationships isn't conducive to having children. The majority of women will, at some stage, want to have a child but the windows of opportunity—when her desire for a child coincides with being in a happy, stable relationship—are not large. And the chances of her wanting a child and having a partner who also wants a child are smaller. And the chances of them both being happy to have a child and their being in the right biological space—to say nothing of the right geographical space and economic circumstances—are even smaller. It's not so much a case of the biological clock ticking but a case of setting everyone's watches to the same time. This conundrum was elegantly expressed by Angie, an email correspondent to the ABC radio program on balancing work and life issues.

I'm going to be lucky if I even get to make a choice between work and kids. I'm 35 years old. My last long-term partner (of more than five years) felt he was 'too young' for children (he's my age). My current long-term partner (again more than five years) and who is just over 40 thinks that he is 'too old'.

One of my old school friends found that her reluctance to commit narrowed her chance of having children later on.

I didn't rush in as I think, being the oldest of 6, I wasn't that keen on surrounding myself with the whole thing again. So, got married at 31, had my son at 36 and then not wanting him to be an only child kept trying . . . and trying . . . and trying! At the age of 44 (with a little help from science) we had two girls. Going from one to three was a BIG change.

Conservative voices like to sheet much of the blame for low fertility to the decline of marriage and they inevitably refer to a golden period of family that occurred sometime around the 50s and 60s. But this conservative pining for a return to their past fails to account for two major considerations. First, we are just emerging from an era of marriage that is unprecedented. The overwhelming dominance of the nuclear family was an aberration of the post-war years. It wasn't the norm between the wars and it wasn't universal among nineteenth-century families. In many ways, the sorts of relationships we have today are a return to normal. But it's a return to the 'normal' of the nineteenth and early twentieth centuries, rather than a return to the 50s. Second, the nature of society demands different roles of us. Globalisation, people's mobility, changes in life stages, the need for knowledge, workplace insecurity and the individualisation of identity all conspire to create different sorts of relationships. The intimate relationships of the world are changing and, while today's university student knows that, her parents don't always appreciate it.

Modern relationships have certainly moved on from the altar-bound stereotype of the 50s. Serious relationships are hard to find and harder still to sustain. Friends have replaced family. Living together doesn't necessarily mean serious intent. And if the urge for something cute emerges, then many will settle for a puppy. The new world of relationships begins in adolescence but extends throughout adult life.

A 'Profile of Young Australians' was drawn in a study released by the Foundation for Young Australians in 2004 and it showed that people up to the age of 24 years are more likely to be raiding the parents' fridge than setting up their own households. Forty-six per cent of people between the ages of 20 and 24 are still living at home. During their early twenties, a quarter of them will move out of home but half of them will move back into the home. The boomerang generation is a product of extended education and the costs of living independently, especially in Australia's capital cities. The majority of children, 75 per cent, stay at school until the end of Year 12 and most of these will go on to university or technical or trade education. And they're not exactly hopping into study with alacrity. The biggest growth of students attending university in 2002 was among 20- to 24-year-olds (up 9 per cent) and the second biggest growth was among 25- to 29-year-olds (up 7 per cent). Youth in rural areas are twice as likely to leave home as their urban mates and most of them converge on capital cities, where education and job opportunities are greater.[1]

The extension of education years has created a long twilight of adolescence and this twilight can sometimes last until the 'child' is 30-plus. One in eight people aged between 25 and 34 years are still at home. This figure is still well below the Italian experience, where the majority of men are living with mama and papa on their 30th birthday—a phenomenon known as il *mammismo* or 'mama's boy'. Indeed, countries with 30-year-old kids living at home are invariably countries with low fertility rates. Italy, Spain and Greece all have very low birth levels and big populations of 'il *mammismo*'. In Italy 71 per cent of 20- to 29-year-olds still live with their parents, in Spain 59 per cent of 20-somethings live at home and in Greece 49 per cent are at home throughout their twenties.

By comparison, countries with reasonable levels of fertility have kissed their adult boarders goodbye. In Sweden only 18 per cent of 20-somethings live with their parents, in the UK 19 per cent, in Denmark the figure is 27 per cent and in France it's 33 per cent. In Japan, home of the 'parasitic single', 80 per cent of single women aged in their twenties are still at home and 70 per cent of those aged 30 to 34 are at home. Offspring who leave home late in their adult lives don't have the time to start their own families—by the time many of them find a life-long partner and think about having children many will only have a few years left on their biological calendar. And perhaps they also don't have the inclination to start their own family if they are getting the love, nurturing and laundry duties from their own parents.

In a demographic sense, parents who keep their children at home well into their adult years are loving their children to death.

Most parents in the developed world discourage children from entering life-long relationships too early or having children young— if only because many of them got hitched too early. And most of the children agree with them. As one of my school friends said:

I warn my girls about early pregnancies and I tell them to think of careers, travel etc. We are not ready to be grandparents yet!

Again, in that 'Profile of Young Australians', only 8 per cent of 17- and 18-year-olds want to marry within five years. For the vast majority of teenagers, marriage is something they don't want to engage in until they are over the age of 25. This is not just a turnaround on the 50s, when most women who were going to be married had hitched up by their 25th birthday, it's a major turnaround in attitudes from 20-odd years ago. In 1981, 80 per cent of young women wanted to be a bride in their early twenties, now only 37 per cent want that. Their expectations of when and whether they want children have changed just as radically. Only 10 per cent of 17- and 18-year-olds want a child before they're 25. The vast majority of women aged eighteen to 23 (92 per cent) want to have had a child by their 35th birthday. But the reality is that only 78 per cent of them will have children by then. In between the hopes of young women and the reality of mid-thirties women, lies a world of travel, careers, independent lifestyles and a tapestry of relationships.

On average, people today are getting hitched six years later than their parents. In 1971, the median age for brides was 21 and for grooms 23, while in 2001, it was 27 for brides and 29 for grooms. But fewer people are choosing marriage and fewer are staying married. De facto partnerships, once considered a shabby form of marriage, now account for one in ten 'socially married' relationships (although they are legally recognised). Many more people across the whole of society are electing to either 'try out' their relationship before marriage or permanently settle into a de facto relationship. Certainly, the numbers who are trying out the relationship has rocketed. In 1981 less than a third of people lived together before marriage; in 2001 two-thirds gave marriage a trial.

Much debate in conservative circles has centred on whether these 'pseudo' forms of marriage are undermining the institution of marriage and family. Certainly, marriage isn't as popular but de facto relationships aren't what they used to be and both marriage and de facto relationships are more unstable. In 2001, Australia's crude marriage rate was the lowest on record and about half what it was in the years after World War II. On international comparisons, it's still above most marriage rates in Europe but below the US rate. But Australia's modern coyness about the institution of marriage is on par with what it was like at the turn of the twentieth century. This historical perspective was explored in a publication from the Australian Institute of Family Studies by Michael Gilding in his 2001 paper, 'Changing Families in Australia, 1901–2001'.

> *There is a sense in which family structure has gone a full circle—from diverse families, to nuclear families and back to diverse families again . . . We can see the same ebb and flow in marriage. One hundred years ago, there was widespread delayed marriage, and marriage was far from universal.*[2]

As the paper points out, at the turn of the twentieth century, one in ten households had servants living with them and another 10 per cent had a lodger; many more had extended family living with them—grandparents, cousins etc. In those days, it was accepted that a certain proportion of women would be 'maiden aunts', who would eschew marriage and spend their lives looking after their parents. There was also a coterie of career women who, naturally, would also avoid marriage. And there were large populations of 'gay bachelors'—these included city blokes with gadfly lifestyles and especially rural men, whose work took them around the countryside and largely away from home and hearth.

The biggest difference between the relationship profiles of 100 years ago and those of today is the high rate of divorce. By the turn of the 21st century there were 1.1 million divorced people in

Australia's population of 15.4 million adults. The divorce rate is roughly half the marriage rate and for many couples divorce interrupts family formation or wipes out plans for a family altogether. But another study done at the Australian Institute of Family Studies, shows that de facto relationships are also more prone to breakdowns. This 2001 paper titled, 'Changing Patterns of Relationship Formation', studied four groups of women, the youngest of whom were aged 25 to 29 years and the oldest 40 to 44 years. The older two groups of women had begun living with a man at earlier ages and their relationships were much more likely to end up in marriage than in the removalist's van—only 10 per cent split up after four years. However, the younger group of women split up with their partners three times more often than the older women. The authors suggest that the greater volatility of de facto relationships is due to the fact that younger women enter these relationships earlier and more lightly than their older sisters did. Or maybe they are just choosier. The authors said:

> Cohabitation was predominantly a prelude to marriage for women born in the early 1950s, and appears to have become progressively less so for younger generations . . . Possibly young couples today may be more likely to cohabit at an earlier stage in their relationship, when 'going steady', rather than when considering marriage. Alternatively, young couples may now embark on cohabitation as a 'trial marriage' but hold higher expectations about having their needs fulfilled in the relationship and be more prepared to separate if their needs are not met.[3]

So, more women are spending time in relationships that don't head towards the altar, the mortgage belt or the maternity ward. This might not be the failure or tragedy that it seems. As the authors suggest, living-together relationships mean different things to the younger generation. It might be a way to save money for a couple who are just dating. It's reasonably common for loosely tied couples to live together when overseas for convenience sake. Certainly, it's become common for couples to continue to live together even though they recognise the relationship won't progress—often because it's too expensive to live apart. And there are endless anecdotes about couples who stay together hoping to change the other person's idea about having or not having children. Still, as far as reproduction goes, more women are spending more of their biologically powerful years in dead-end relationships. Some will emerge from these relationships to find that their biological clock is on count-down, others come out of relationships with one child and will never have another one. The volatility of relationships mucks up life plans and family planning. One of my school friends commented:

> Divorce is far easier today than it was 30 years ago and I think this would also have an influence on the number of children. I'm divorced so don't know if I had remained married if there would have been any more children. Perhaps that's what women did years ago if they were unhappy, have more kids for someone to love.

The difference between those who are voluntarily childless and those who are there by default is fuzzier than ever. Some who end up childless always wanted it that way but many more may have wanted children at one stage of their life, or with one certain partner. Having children may have been a dream for 30 years or 30 minutes. A lifetime of not wanting children might be over-turned at the last moment.

The commitment-shy bachelor is the archetypal villain of family life. He is the bastard of chick lit, he's the lovable rogue of sit coms and he sometimes cops it between the eyes from conservative politicians. There aren't many comprehensive surveys on why some men avoid or delay commitments (getting them to sit down for a good chat is something their girlfriends can't manage either). Still the surveys that have been done indicate that men aren't under the same social pressure to marry as they once were and they don't think as highly of the institution of marriage. A survey by Relationships Australia in 1998 showed the main reasons men and women list for not getting married were fear of divorce (30 per cent), to avoid commitment (26 per cent), the fear of making a mistake (25 per cent), a previous bad experience (23 per cent) and the idea that strong commitment doesn't need marriage (23 per cent). A similar survey was done in the United States among men only in 2002 by the Rutgers University National Marriage Project (a conservative think tank). The reasons men aged 25 to 33 give for remaining footloose reflect a rationalist approach to marriage rather than a romantic one. The top five reasons were: they can get sex without marriage; they can enjoy the benefits of having a wife by cohabiting; they want to avoid divorce; they want to wait until they are older to have children and they fear marriage would require too many changes and compromises.

Whether it's because of commitment-phobic men or the influence of the independent woman, relationships are looser. The young married folk of the 70s and 80s thought it was a big deal to write their own wedding ceremonies. The couples of today are writing their own scripts for living together. They're living in collaborative couplings, mutually convenient relationships and til-boredom-do-us-part arrangements.

This more casual approach towards relationships was encountered by social researcher Hugh Mackay, in his 1997 book, *Generations*. Examining different attitudes among generations, he found that those born in the 70s liked to keep their options open.

'For the Options Generations,' he wrote, '"happy marriage" might well mean "ten years of happiness", it might mean a short or long period of cohabitation—with or without the tying of a legal knot—or it might mean a life-long commitment to one partner. The ideal marriage, for the rising generation, is sometimes described as "being married to my best friend".'4

If marriage and de facto relationships are more lightweight, then the world of dating is positively ephemeral. In 2003, one of my daughters began using the term 'hook-up' to describe goings-on in her group. In her words a hook-up 'might mean you kissed them or it might mean you had sex with them but it at least involves tongue and it doesn't mean that much'.5 As the parent of a teenage girl, it was hard for me to know how to take that. Concentrate on the tongue bit, I guess. But that expression, which was common around the world, seemed to encapsulate many of the qualities of modern sexual relationships. First, the definition was loose—open to interpretation—but second, the nature of the relationship was casual. A hook-up is both predatory and dismissive. At the same time that hook-up became a popular expression, New York women started referring to their 'sometimes boyfriend'. The sometimes boyfriend would fly into town for a few days, squire the girl around and when he flew off the girlfriend would be left with broken sleep but no baggage.

Internet dating was also taking singles into a world of click-on lovers. Sometimes, those screen dalliances brought together people who lived on opposite sides of the country or the world—creating a new form of migratory bird sweeping across the globe. Another fad was speed dating—a method of courting that bypassed expensive cocktails with a five-minute interview. For younger age groups, traffic light parties became the rage—wear red if you're taken, green if you're available and orange if you're unsure (orange has always been a difficult colour). These dating fashions captured the momentum of the times—they used technology, speed, business-like arrangements and low-risk analysis. As Jerry Seinfeld said in an episode on dating: 'Dating is pressure and tension. What is a date really but a job interview that lasts all night? The only difference between a date and a job interview is that in not too many job interviews is there a chance you'll end up naked at the end of it.'

While many have called this generation's flightiness a long twilight of adolescence or 'adulescence', educationalist Johanna Wyn believes it is a new form of adulthood. She is the director at Melbourne University's Australian Youth Research Centre and has followed the lives of 2000 Australians from when they left school in 1991. By 2004, most were turning 30 and they weren't in any mood for settling down. Only a third were married and only 13 per cent had children. Older generations still look at these 20- and 30-somethings and wonder when they'll settle down to the sort of lives they had, the sort of life they consider is part of the natural order.

But Wyn's research indicates that adulthood isn't being delayed, it's being fundamentally changed. As she writes in her book, Youth and Society:

> Rather than creating an extended period of youth, their lives and perspectives suggest that they are entering adulthood incrementally earlier than previous generations. During their late teens and early 20s, young people are forging adult patterns of life that will endure into their 30s and 40s, characterised by juggling multiple responsibilities, job mobility, engaging in life-long learning and an emphasis on their personal development and autonomy.[6]

The generation that swapped dating for hook-ups, that preferred friends to fiancés and that stayed at home until their parents' patience ran out, is building a new world of relationships. What you see is what they're likely to be tomorrow.

These fluid relationships may be their choice, but as the expression 'sometimes boyfriend' implies, they are often the result of the increased mobility across the country and across the world.

We live in mobile times. In the 90s, Australians became some of the most mobile people in the world. Between 1991 and 1994, 43 per cent of Australians, youth in particular, moved house. In the five years to 2001, 64 per cent of people in their early twenties moved, and one in ten of these moved interstate. Rural youth were twice as likely to shift house and two-thirds of these moved to capital cities.

Nowadays, with globalisation, we are also shifting around the world. At any one time there are one million Australians living overseas and most of those are in their twenties and thirties. Shifting house, especially if it's across the world, disrupts established relationships and, often, delays family formation.

A less obvious impact of our itinerant lifestyles is how it takes couples away from the emotional supports of family. As a school friend said in my mini-poll of the class of 74:

> For me, having supportive parents and extended family has been a definite bonus in raising a family while simultaneously pursuing a career. My adult children, however, cannot see themselves having children any time soon because of the high cost of housing and child care in Sydney.

The role of grandparents in facilitating the birth of the next generation is often underestimated. According to Australian Bureau of Statistics figures, a quarter of children under the age of four years are regularly cared for by grandparents. The benefit of the presence of grandparents isn't just in free child care. A study produced at the

University of Turku in Finland and published in *Nature* magazine in 2004 found that the presence of grandmothers allowed their offspring 'to breed earlier, more frequently and more successfully'. Studying families from the eighteenth and nineteenth century in Finland and Canada, the researchers found that women whose mothers were still alive had more children—up to two more children—and raised more of them to maturity. When the grandmother lived more than twenty kilometres away, fewer children were produced. The researchers speculate that the supportive role of grandparents gave their children an advantage in procreating the next generation.[7]

The role of the extended family, however, is being eroded by aging and geographic movements. Not only are young people moving around the globe, older people are making sea changes of their own. In Australia the shift to the coast by 55- to 70-year-olds is literally robbing many young—or, at least, new—families of crucial support. The aging of motherhood is obviously resulting in an aging of grandparents. As a 30-something comedian said a few years ago, 'I want to have children before my mum's too old to look after them'. When women had children in their twenties, their mothers were likely to be fit, active, middle-aged women. When they have their babies in their late thirties, their grandparents are likely to be 65 years and older—not so able to withstand the energies of a toddler or two. Said one of my school mums:

> Older parents means older grandparents and, speaking personally, my parents are too old to look after the kids or do anything physical with them. My mother dearly wishes she was young enough to be a 'proper' grandmother.

We live in lonely times. One in four households has just one person and this could rise to one in three within fifteen years. The rise of the lone householder has been one of the biggest stories in housing and the property market over the past two decades. So too has the decline in the classical family home. From 1976 to 2001, the proportion of all houses that were occupied by a couple with children dropped from 60 per cent to 41 per cent. You can, literally, see the result of these demographic movements in the skyline of modern cities like Sydney, where 15 per cent of dwellings are apartments and 10 per cent are town houses. This shift to living alone or living with just one other person is both cosmopolitan and modern. In 1911, when there were still high proportions of single men and single women, few people lived alone, if only because there wasn't the sort of housing to accommodate them. The average number of people living in a house has shrunk from 4.5 people in 1911, to 2.6 people and it's estimated to shrink again to about 2.2 within the next decade or so. In new unit complexes there are as many bathrooms as there are bedrooms and in middle-class housing developments there are usually *more* bathrooms than bedrooms. We are actually creating more toilets than children.

Home design often mirrors how we think about the family and what our aspirations are. Relationships are reflected in the bricks and mortar we build around them. From a town planning perspective, many young people in Australia look at the vast expanse of suburbia and shudder. Whereas twenty years ago there wasn't such a gulf between sharing a house in inner suburbia with friends and sharing a house in outer suburbia with a family, today's single living in an inner city apartment can barely see the horizons of the suburbia that is traditionally regarded as the place of families. The suburban estate with the freestanding houses, car access and community that could only be found in a distant mall, was meant to be the family dream.

But after decades of greenfield developments there is growing recognition that this sort of town planning doesn't appeal much to modern families. It's easy to see the suburban estate as reflecting the thinking of the 50s patriarchy—dad drives off to work in the morning, leaving mum and the kids isolated in a neat, brick house. Mum and the toddlers might be able to escape to the mall to shop but there is little in the way of entertainment, education or civic activities within reach. Bricks and mortar sometimes stand as testimony to social conventions that have moved on.

There are signs that modern families are carving niches in the landscape to suit their values. Some are moving out and some are staying in. A significant proportion of the sea-change movement is composed of young families who are shifting outside cities, in search of both better lifestyles and cheaper housing. Many of these families set up telecommuting operations with city businesses, they travel to work in the outer areas of the city or they set up their own small businesses. More families are also choosing to remain in the inner city when they have young children, rather than take that well-trod path to the burbs. In inner city areas, such as Alexandria in Sydney, the proportion of young families has grown steadily as more chose a European-style of living, with smaller homes but greater use of public parks, cafes, galleries and entertainment options. But for many more middle-income and lower-income groups, the alternative to life in suburbia is a rental pad. For both young singles and young couples the cost of a mortgage is out of reach. Home ownership for young couples fell from 60 per cent to 52 per cent in just the five years to 1999. The decade-long property boom has made home ownership least affordable for those who may be thinking of having children. For the majority of young people in Australia, owning their own home is still seen as a precursor to family life. Whether this idea is historical, cultural or biological, it is an enduring one: that you must buy the home and then have the family. The high cost of housing in cities is forcing many young couples to give up on the idea of owning a home, or move out of their birthplaces, or give up on the idea of family, or delay it for so long that they're not going to have time for many children.

So who ends up alone and often childless? Part of the answer is still the well-educated city woman. But the woman who cries, 'Oh no, I forgot to have children' at age 40 isn't the only one. A study titled 'Men and Women Apart', mentioned earlier, showed that in the past fifteen years there has been a large increase in numbers of men and women who fail to find partners. These are mainly those with only high school education. This reflects both a growing population of singles across society but also an increasing marriage gap. There are educated women who can't find enough 'good' men to marry, but there are many more men whose low incomes make them unattractive partners, even to women of their own socio-economic class.[8]

The overall decline is seen in the fact that in the fifteen years to 2001, the number of women aged 20 to 24 years with partners dropped 15 per cent; and for women aged 25 to 29 years it dropped 14 per cent. The figures for marriages shrank even more sharply. The number of women aged 25 to 29 years who were married dropped from 61 per cent to 37 per cent.

Educated women in their early thirties are now less likely to have partners than they were in the 80s. The problem for well-educated women who are looking for a partner of their socio-economic class is partly a result of the fact that there are more well-educated women than men. For the educated 20-something woman the successful search for a university graduate partner has roughly the same odds as a coin throw. The report points out that when it comes to their late twenties, there are 40 per cent more well-educated women than there are well-educated men. The women who sat in university lecture halls in the 80s and 90s could see their dating future in the number of blokes sitting in the same hall—it didn't take a PhD to appreciate that when the music stopped there would be a lot of women left standing.

The single life is also becoming much more common for women without post-school education. Between 1986 and 2001, the percentage of these women who were in partnerships in their early thirties dropped from 77 per cent to 65 per cent. The stereotypical idea that women who are less educated and therefore more likely to have duller jobs will leap into marriage is no longer holding true. But, according to the authors, the most alarming drop in partnering rates is among the new under-class of men—those who have neither high education levels nor incomes to attract a mate and start a family. The percentage of high school educated men in their early thirties who have partners has dropped from 68 per cent to 52 per cent. The authors argue that while the single, successful woman may be alone because of either a numerical lack of suitable partners or lifestyle considerations, the single, low-income man is alone because of the economic shifts of the past decade:

> Though they seem to accept their fate stoically, low income men are the big losers in the partnering stakes . . . To be at the bottom of the income scale is bad enough in a consumerist society. But, in addition, their financial circumstances contribute to their inability to achieve a key marker of manhood. That is, the creation and maintenance of a new household.[9]

This image of the low-income, less-educated and often insecure worker who cannot find a partner is redolent of the image of the early-twentieth-century itinerant man who takes to the road to pick up jobs and gives up the idea of a family. As the report points out, there was the same percentage (40 per cent) of unmarried men in their late twenties in 1911 as in 2001. Similarly, there is something reminiscent in the well-educated, modern city women who can't find a mate of those well-bred maiden aunts of a previous century who ended up looking after elderly parents rather than make a bad match. But, while the outcomes are similar, there is a world of difference in the forces that led these women and men there and which affected the many different relationships they had along the way.

There is also, we hope, a better way of responding to the breakdown in modern relationships than the way found a century ago. As Michael Gilding's article on families from 1901 to 2001 pointed out, the decline in late-nineteenth-century births sparked a moral panic. In 1903 a Royal Commission on the Decline of the Birth Rate and on the Mortality of Infants was set up in NSW. In its report, the Commission refuted the suggestion that people couldn't afford to raise a large number of children and said it was more of a result of 'selfishness'. It was, the Commission declared, the result of women's 'unwillingness to [accept] physical discomfort, the strain and worry associated with child-bearing and child-rearing and a love of luxury and social pleasures'.[10]

Carefree singles and careless parents

One night I passed by the television set while my daughters were watching *Sex and the City*. I didn't approve of the viewing and the girls didn't approve of my presence. They prefer to get their information on the protocol of farting in bed while their mother is out of the room. At one point in this episode, the main character, Carrie, lamented, 'I have spent money on wedding presents and on other people's children and no one has ever celebrated the fact that I am single'. Oh, but they have, Carrie, they have.

Every week of the television season from 1998 to 2004, *Sex and the City* celebrated the single life—from the etiquette of oral sex and faking orgasm to choosing/losing/loving Manolo Blahnik sling-backs. Every week from 1994 to 2004, *Friends* toasted the single life around their shared apartments, the Fooz-ball table and the couch in the Central Perk cafe. Every week between 1991 and 1998 *Seinfeld* tracked the single life problems of how to dump girlfriends, how to split a bill and how to handle a Pez dispenser. And in other television time slots of the 90s and the early years of the 21st century we caught Ally McBeal as the single, career woman, Frasier as the urbane bachelor and Will and Grace juggling the lifestyles of the gay man and the unattached woman. Then, of course, there were the other carefree (and mostly single) series of *Thirtysomething*, *Charmed*, *Buffy the Vampire Slayer*, *Melrose Place*, *Queer as Folk*, *Becker*, plus the plethora of reality dating shows, *Survivor* shows and *Big Brother* households that featured the young and the lithe.

Everyone has their fifteen minutes of fame but singles and the childless have had fifteen years of fame. From the turn of the 90s, television screens around the world turned their backs on family, kids, youth and oldies and embraced the 18- to 35-year-old demographic. What was niche television in the 80s—think *Murphy Brown* and *Moonlighting*—became mainstream in the 90s. The single life was no longer subsidiary, sad or something to be resolved in a wedding. It was an end in itself. The status of singles was so enhanced during this era that the oldest character in *Sex and the City*, Samantha, could end the series saying, 'I'm forty-fucking-five and proud of it' and have a large part of New York, London, Sydney, Hong Kong and Perth thanking her for it.

Proud, funny, feisty and . . . over?

Sex and the City, *Friends* and *Frasier* all ended in 2004. They were still hugely successful when they took their bows, so why did they end? Sure, the actors were getting weary of the roles and there wasn't much left in a dramatic sense that Carrie, Samantha, Charlotte, Miranda, Frasier, Joey, Rachel, Ross, Phoebe, Monica and Chandler hadn't already done. But there was a more compelling reason to take these singles off the screen. They were aging. They might not have grown up—hell, they were still holding arm-wrestling competitions—but they were getting on in years.

Watching a 45-year-old Samantha play predatory sex games doesn't quite have the same cachet as seeing a 30-year-old woman on the prowl. Joey's excitement about getting another bit part in a commercial falls flatter as he reaches his late thirties. These small screen idols may have helped extend adolescence to the cusp of middle age but even they had to finally face the prospect of life beyond the cafe. At a certain age, youth passes—it might be 20, 30 or 40 years of age—but at that stage a person will look around and think, 'What comes next?'. Unfortunately for the cast of singles television series and the population of urban sophisticates who celebrated their lives in their own living rooms, by the time they turn around and ask 'What comes next?', one of those options is almost closed to them.

It wasn't just network television that took singles and the childless out of the closet and into an extended celebration. The carefree life was reflected in books, news media, design, entertainment and retailing. After the publication of *Bridget Jones' Diary*, a new genre, chick lit, emerged to engage with the major preoccupations of intelligent, sassy, single women. Unlike the desperate and dateless story of Bridget Jones, much of the subsequent literature tended to celebrate the single life. As the titles of the top sellers' lists indicate, the chick lit genre swayed between sex lives—*Loose Screws, So Long Mr Wrong, Mr Right for the Night*—and stilettos lifestyles—*Running in Heels, Simply Divine* and *The Cinderella Rules*. The lads didn't miss out either. The emergence of 'lad lit' in the form of *Men Behaving Badly, Fight Club* and *High Fidelity* chronicled the tales of modern men caught in bad habits and dodgy jobs. The commitment-phobic bloke was as prominent as ever in popular culture and imagination but in many ways, he wasn't the issue. To be coy about commitment implies that women are keen to commit and increasingly they weren't. Throughout the past fifteen years, the society image of single sophisticates moved beyond the whining Bridget Jones to the single-not-worried Carrie and her mates.

The successful singles became one of the most lucrative target markets for media and products. In the daily news media, they found new magazine inserts in newspapers that chronicled the lifestyles of bar flies and fly-buys. The market for boys' toys boomed on the back of 30-something adulescents—X-boxes, Fooz ball tables, scooters, convertibles, dune buggies, water scooters and high-performance bikes. The 90s and the early 21st century was a time of vodka cocktails, bars with million-dollar makeovers, adventure travel for singles, SMS conversations, Saturday mornings in the cafe and single-serve gourmet meals. Retailers began reconfiguring their stock and service levels to cater to the cashed-up, time-poor, single. Supermarkets introduced lines of single serve meals and snacks to catch the 'two-bag shopper' who descended on stores at 7 p.m. Property developers talked of building apartment blocks without kitchens—just heat and serve centres. One of the popular messages on the front of women's t-shirts in 2004 said:

I think

Therefore

I'm single

The 90s was a good time to be single and young(ish). As Joseph Epstein wrote in the US national magazine the *Weekly Standard* in 2004, 'Youth is no longer viewed as a transitory state, through which one passes on the way from childhood to adulthood, but an aspiration, a vaunted condition in which, if one can only manage it, to settle in perpetuity'.[1]

The culture of carefree was both a reflection of the changing demographics and a feeder of the trend. Young people from country areas and from around the world were descending on cities for jobs, lifestyles, education and cultural experiences. Their convergence meant the average age in cities like Sydney and Melbourne was a year or two lower than other areas of the continent; their presence rejuvenated suburbs like Bondi and St Kilda as daggy flats were given minimalist make-overs; and their mobility redefined town planning theories. It was a global movement of talent, energy and attitude that American academic Richard Florida captured in his book, *The Rise of the Creative Class*. This book argued that it was no longer industry, trade or natural resources that determined a city's economic status but people and, in particular, creative people. Cities that attracted gays, bohemians, graduates and creative workers were becoming the hothouses of 21st century economies.[2] The young and restless were reinventing the world.

This class of freewheeling spirits, who roved the *uber* centres of the world in search of experience, was also described in a book called *Hub Culture*. As its author, Stan Stalnaker, wrote:

> *We are only now seeing the rise of a new global class that can move between any number of cities with ease. It is a group of people that job hunt on a global basis . . . live through phone lists and email databases . . . they are the common market and they span the world.*
>
> *Young and cynical, affluent but cash poor, they are at a nice moment in life—experienced enough to know it's the same everywhere but still curious enough to want to know what else there is. They are consumed by the quest for experience.[3]*

But one experience they were not keen on is parenthood. As Stalnaker says, the four major varieties of relationships found among the globals were: bi-cultural marriage (to heighten the cultural experience), long-term monogamous relationships, serial long-distance relationships and single-not-worried status.

Were we seeing a new tribe? A new class? A new age of adulthood? Or the delusion of a generation? An American author, Ethan Watters, called it a tribe and intimated it might also be a delusion. In his book, *Urban Tribes*, Watters recounted the extended adolescence enjoyed by himself and his friends, who were mostly white, well-educated Americans, whose only thought of the future was how soon they would inherit. As he wrote, 'Why worry about saving for retirement when your parents have done it for you?' The book comprised interviews and research, but mostly first-hand accounts of a tribe that were so close they dined together weekly, went to festivals together, shared apartments, worked on projects jointly and vetted each other's romantic interests.[4] Although Watters' gang members were obviously cushioned from economic reality, their attitudes were reflected throughout the generation of 20- to 40-year-olds in those fifteen years to 2005.

This was the *Friends* generation—young adults who built a family of friends rather than build their own families. For the baby boom generation, there was often only a few years from when they left their birth families to when they found a partner with whom they would build their own families. The next generation, however, would often spend a decade, or two, in the company of close friends. Partners would come and go but the friends remained the constant support, sharing outings, apartments, dramas, jobs and travels and, often, a distaste for settling down. A constant refrain from the carefree single was that they didn't want to 'waste' the best years of their life. This is a refrain that's familiar to the women of the baby boom generation. The boomers looked at the lives of their mothers—caught at home with children and chores—and swore they wouldn't waste their life in the confines of motherhood. The next generation looked at their mothers and swore they wouldn't waste the best years of their life doing the double shift of work and family. The message that having children is a 'waste' of time—a waste that is only tolerable when the best years of life are finished—is remarkably persistent.

Interestingly, Watters wrote the book after he'd married and had a child. It was a safe territory from which to view friends who, he wrote, try not to think of the future but find that 'with each passing year, the pressure builds a little'.

Globals, who turn grey before they grow up, helped to set the tone of an era. For many 20-somethings and 30-somethings, the lifestyle of *Friends* was fun to watch, but it was often the default position in their own lives. Locked out of the home ownership market by high prices and forced into a series of revolving jobs by the greater insecurity in the workforce, many young adults were effectively forced into the no-cares, no-commitments life. Educationalist, Johanna Wyn, who has followed the lives of 2000 young Australians at the Australian Research Centre, says many youth are surprised that they're still footloose at the age of 30. In an interview for this book, she says, many thought they would have got it sorted by 30, however, only a third of them were married and only 13 per cent had had a child. Insecure jobs and nomadic lives, she says, have taught this generation 'that they must be responsive and flexible. The best scenario for them is to have the option to move on and shape their lives around uncertainty.'[5] If the popular media wasn't turning them into nomads, then the economy was and the combination of economic hardball and social stereotyping helped build a sense of identity. How much they influenced decisions made by their generation is impossible to say. But, as Malcolm Gladwell wrote in The Tipping Point, it isn't just children who are shaped by their environment. 'The features of our immediate social and physical world—the streets we walk down, the people we encounter—play a huge role in shaping who we are and how we act.

It isn't just serious criminal behaviour, in the end, that is sensitive to environmental cues, it is all behaviour.'[6]

Gladwell's book explored how the forces of role modelling, word-of-mouth and social context can create a fashion fad, a health epidemic or social revolutions. The same forces that push Hush Puppies into a sudden revival or clean up New York's street crime or lure people into gentrifying suburbs, can lead to an explosion of singleness. In the past, cultural pressures have also led to epidemics of children. It was powerful media, government and commercial pressures that created the stay-at-home mum of the 50s. In the 90s and 2000s, the epidemic of singleness was fed by media, economic pressures, peer group lifestyles and popular culture. From the perspective of the young of that era, nobody seemed to be having children.

Identifying the 'tipping point' at which the single life became a movement is near impossible—it might have been the start of *Seinfeld*, it could have been the launch of the Razor scooter or the first party that was arranged on a 'cc' email list. Finding the point at which it tips back—if it does—will be just as tricky. You have to wonder about those friends of Ethan Watters, reading about their late-stage adolescence in a bestselling book written by a friend who has made the leap into commitment. You've got to admire Samantha from *Sex and the City* declaring she is 'forty-fucking-five' and loving it, but you also wonder how many other 45-year-old single sophisticates say the same. You may also wonder about the end of *Friends*. After a pyjama party that lasted a decade, they suddenly found themselves closing in on their 40th birthday. And what did a quarter of the population of the United States see when the final episode gave everyone closure? The friends opted for domestic bliss and finally left the dorm for the proverbial burbs. Phoebe was married and planning a child, Chandler and Monica had taken off to the country with their bubs and Rachel leapt off the plane to Paris into the arms of the father of her baby, Ross. Only Joey was left to carry the banner for singles and for a new series.

The single life needed renovation. Previous eras have been cruel to single people, labelling them selfish or gallivants or losers. In the 80s, it was said that a single woman of 40 had more chance of being targeted by a terrorist than a groom—and that was before September 11. But the renovation of the single life was done partly at the expense of family life. You don't have to have been a regular TV viewer to appreciate how deeply unfashionable family life became since 1990 but a quick look at the schedule may help. The top family shows from America have been *Malcolm in the Middle*, *Roseanne*, *Home Improvement*, *The Sopranos*, *Everyone Loves Raymond* and *The Simpsons*. In short, they encompass boys with pathologies, housewife shrews, cuddly murderers, in-laws from hell and dead-beat but lovable dads. And most of the series are set in Copper-art homes, with wardrobes of bum-crack pants and the sort of energy that's reserved for a Saturday afternoon snooze. Viewed from the television couch, the world of families and the world of singles were on different planets— and they weren't Mars and Venus. If singles were the sun of our universe, then the family was on Pluto. And there wasn't much love between the two ends of the solar system. Indeed, societal scorn, once reserved for singles, switched to families and particularly to mothers.

One episode of *The Simpsons* that cropped up in 2004 explored some of the antagonism that was developing between singles and families. The episode started off with a babies' rock concert that gets out of hand. A town meeting is held to discuss the 'Tot Offensive' and the fact that the town is expected to pay for the damage wrought by tots and babies. Lindsay Nagle addresses the meeting on behalf of SSCCTGAPP (Singles, Seniors, Childless Couples, Teenagers and

Gays Against Parasitic Parents) and has a Martin Luther King moment on stage. 'I dream of an America with nudity and F words on network TV, where the whole world doesn't stop because a school bus did. Children are the future, today belongs to me!' She then says, 'Let's kill every child-friendly thing in town.' Marge, in typical mother mode, attempts to assuage Lindsay by introducing her to the ideal child, Lisa. 'I bought with me the very best reason I could think of for what I believe in,' says Marge. 'Her name is Lisa and I wouldn't trade her for all the sleep-in Sundays and speed dating in the world.' Lindsay casts her eye over Lisa and declares, 'I would be proud if one of the eggs I sold turned out like you.'[7]

The childless lobby was a small but increasingly vocal minority through the 90s and into the 21st century. One of the most popular of the groups is called No Kidding and another American group goes by the anagram, THINKERS (Two Healthy Incomes, No Kids, Early Retirement). In 2000, a Sydney couple, Susan and David Moore, published *Child-Free Zone*—which was an account of their reasons and those of 80 childless couples they interviewed for not having children. The book recounted the frustration of childless couples coming up against societal pressures to procreate, putting up with other people's children in public spaces and seeing their taxes support children that other people choose to have. As they said:

> *Many child-free people resent the fact that they are forever paying for services they will never need and, at worst, for other people's lack of forethought and planning (especially family planning). Some also believe they should be compensated for their lack of reliance on government funds.*[8]

But the family didn't need a child-free lobby, or Lindsay from *The Simpsons* or a television tribe of friends to know it was on the nose.

Parents just had to pick up a newspaper and read about the killer blaming his mother for his dysfunctional life, or tune into the current affairs program for an encounter with dead-beat dads. Mothers just had to pick up literature on attention deficit disorder or obesity to find out they weren't doing as good a job as their mothers did. Fathers could rely on radio's shock jocks for a bollocking on how they weren't disciplining their children or they could listen to a politician castigating them for not reading to their children. Parents could listen in to water cooler conversations in the office about mothers who snuck out early or dads who never went home. The same society that was celebrating the quirky lives of singles was castigating the family for all its foibles.

And it was happening on a personal level, not just on the political one. I remember walking past a TAFE on the way to work when I was pregnant. Suddenly a young lad came out of the college and said to me, 'You're not meant to wear high heels when you're pregnant!' Never before had a stranger—a young man—made it his job to inform me of what I shouldn't be wearing. And I was wearing pumps, not high heels! (note the defensive tone). His comment stayed with me, not because it was wrong, not even because it was the first piece of sartorial advice I've received from a boy, but because it was the first of many such comments. When I became pregnant, I became public property, a societal concern. Many other women comment on how intrusive people can be when they spot a pregnant tummy or a babe in arms. Much of this is affectionate and well intended but it reinforces the idea that women who become mothers are public property. (How would that TAFE lad feel if I yelled out to him that he should pull his jeans up so his undies didn't show?)

Societies will always feel protective of the next generation but for most parents today society's response to them is negative, carping and often ignorant. Moreover, for new parents the criticism they face from society comes as a shock after the carte blanche they had when they were singles. As carefree singles, they could do no wrong. They were wooed by employers, targeted by advertisers, celebrated by television series and affirmed by friends. They had freedom of movement, dress and opinions. But, as soon as they became parents, they were 'accomodated' by employers, dismissed by fashionable retailers, bagged by television series and confronted by 19-year-old lads with opinions on what they should wear when pregnant.

The concept of mother blame isn't a new one. It was around for all of the twentieth century as shown in the book, *Bad Mothers: The politics of blame in twentieth-century America*. This collection of essays chronicles the perils of being a mother, from the 1930s when too many were thought to be 'excessively mothering' to the early 1990s when America's fetal rights laws cast mothers as dangerous containers for their own children.[9]

Sheila Kitzinger picked up the refrain in her book, *Ourselves as Mothers*.

> *Open any newspaper and you see that mothers are scapegoats for a wide variety of social ills and developmental difficulties from juvenile delinquency, obesity, anorexia, personality problems, autism, hyperactivity and dyslexia and other learning difficulties through to schizophrenia, teenage promiscuity, adult sexual dysfunction and marital failure, drug addiction and violent crime.*[10]

No doubt mothers were also to blame for the disappearance of testosterone in the world's marine species.

If mothers weren't mucking it up, then they weren't doing enough. By the turn of the century, the Superwoman syndrome had dropped out of the social conversation but it was still there beating in the hearts of Supermums. Barbara Pocock, in *The Work/Life*

Collision, explored how it wasn't just work that was intensified during this period, it was mothering as well. And with women facing an intensification at work as well as an intensification of the things expected of them as mothers, they were bound for an epidemic of guilt. 'Mothers are more likely to see the fault in themselves, attempting to meet their "deficiencies" through super-mothering, than they are to look to their partners or to critically examine the rigidities imposed by their workplaces.'[11]

Expected to work like singles, cook like Nigella, dress like Madonna (in low heels), birth like Sheila Kitzinger, raise kids on Penelope Leach toys, live in houses renovated by Jamie Durie and educate their kids like Aristotle, no wonder mothers feel ambivalent about the demands of parenthood. And not terribly competent about it either. According to a survey by the Australian Childhood Foundation released in 2004, most parents are desperate for help with their parenting roles. Three out of four parents said they struggled to find time to enjoy activities with their children, more than half said they lacked confidence in their parenting skills, 60 per cent said they struggled to discipline their children effectively and 80 per cent wanted more information or support on parenting issues.

Had we become bad mothers and bad fathers? Had we suddenly overnight lost the knack of raising the next generation to maturity? Penguins do it, coyotes do it, celebrities do it, tyrants have done it and, as Britain's Father of the Year, Bob Geldof told the *Australian Women's Weekly*, 'A f**king moron could do it'.[12]

What went wrong? What happened to us between our lives as successful singles and our lives as not-good-enough parents? A clue was given by the authors of *The Mommy Myth*, Susan Douglas and Meredith Michaels, when they outlined 'new momism' in the United States. 'The new momism', they wrote, 'is a set of ideals, norms and practices, most frequently and powerfully represented in the media, that seem on the surface to celebrate motherhood, but which in reality promulgate standards of perfection that are beyond your reach. The new momism is the direct descendant and latest version of what Betty Friedan famously labelled the "feminine mystique" back in the 1960s.'[13]

Parents had, unknowingly, stepped onto a treadmill of continuous failure. The ideal of parenthood was placed so far beyond reach that they were bound to fail—every day in every way. As parents, we'd never be able to read all the books that our kids needed, we'd never find enough organic produce to make a whole meal, or monitor all our kids' Internet journeys, or give them enough classes to uncover their talents, or find enough time to throw a ball with them whenever they slumped by the TV. And we never managed to look like the sort of mum that we saw in magazines at the supermarket checkout. Indeed, when parents looked for role models in the popular media, they found only a parade of celebrities at Hollywood benefits with kids, at lunch, on exclusive island resorts, in lookalike clothes with their tots, at Aspen with their family, at hair product launches and shopping in Soho with tots. But we never saw the children because the photographer was never granted an audience with them. Children in the lives of celebrities were like sacred apparitions—a powerful force, rarely witnessed. The celebrity culture wasn't a child-hating forum, on the contrary, babies were fashionable. It was just all that other stuff that came with babies—stretch marks, safe cars, dirty nappies, early nights, school pick-ups and squeezed schedules—were not part of the story. In our celebrity culture, it was okay to have a baby (singular, rather than plural) but one had to get the figure back pronto or, like Liz Hurley and Catherine Zeta-Jones, answer to the women's magazines. It was okay to have kids, as long as they stayed in the background when the photographer came around, didn't interrupt the film shoot and didn't have a tantrum in front of the paparazzi. Babies were fashionable in the same way push-up bras, botox and P.Diddy were fashionable—all show.

A snapshot of how babies became accessories arose in the 2003–04 fashion year when a number of houses such as Gucci and Dolce & Gabbana featured babies and children in their marketing, and *Vanity Fair* ran 400 pages of moms. The images of stylish toddlers with male models and nude babies with leather-clad female models and Hollywood mums-to-be with haute couture bumps didn't put children on the agenda, it just put them on the accessories list. See stockists.

Not too many witnesses to the celebrity culture stopped to think that if these people were in our face all the time, then how often could they be in their children's face? The nature of celebrity—once thought of as corrosive of children—was being held up as the ideal nurturer of children. I never heard of a journalist who asked Pamela Anderson whether she breastfed her babies with her DD silicon breasts, or whether Madonna showed her toddlers her sex files or how many times John Travolta read to his children while he was on a six-month film shoot. And yet we tortured ourselves with these questions about our own children every day. Society had raised the bar on parenting, the myth of celebrity parents cast us in their shadow, and we could draw only one conclusion: we were losers. And everyone knew it. Especially those carefree singles who were looking our way, wondering what lay beyond the last Fooz ball game.

The gulf between single life and family life has rarely been wider. Society's celebration of the single life and its condemnation of families divided us. On a personal level, the switch from carefree single to careless parent happened overnight. On a social level, it happened over a decade and a half.

The irony of the single-life society was that the fun and games they annexed had once belonged to the life of children. That Fooz ball table in the 'Friends' apartment was once found in fun parlours for kids. Those X-boxes that were snapped up by many 30-year-old lads, were designed with a nine-year-old in mind. The media had, in effect, taken the story of childhood and retold it through the lives of adults. When you thought of cute girls, you thought of Rachel; if you spotted a boy with puppy-dog eyes, it was likely to be Ross and if you wanted a fairy princess story—the one where the ugly/abused girl finally gets recognition and revenge—you went to chick lit.

Meanwhile, children were presented as an anchor on lifestyles. They were maybe cute enough, but their impact on the lives of parents was devastating. You just had to look at *Malcolm in the Middle*'s parents to see the damage. Or you could tune into the new genre of teenage movies—*Mean Girls, Bully, Cruel Intentions*—to see how bitchy, materialistic and ruthless kids were by the age of fourteen or fifteen. Perhaps the entertainment media was just reflecting the mood in the family home but, as PR, it pushed family life out of the prime time of the mind.

Popular culture gave us carefree singles, careless parents and children as chores. Someone forgot to remind the young that being with children is also fun. Or maybe they just weren't listening. Then again, society's reconstruction of the family was making us all forget that it's meant to be fun.

Children:
All work, no play

When my son was a skateboarding fiend at the age of eleven, a local council was in the middle of a fight about whether a skateboarding park should be built in the area. One of the wealthiest local councils in the country, Mosman Council, hosted stormy meetings between parents who wanted the facility for their kids and residents who argued it would introduce vandalism, bad behaviour and undesirable types into the area.

As I trooped around to various Sydney skateboarding parks with Toby, I found that the kids at these concrete bowls had an elaborate civil code of behaviour. With ages ranging from seven to seventeen and abilities ranging from beginner to radical, the kids shared these small bowls with an informal set of road rules that any transport minister would be proud of. The youngest kids gave way to the older kids, the inexperienced stuck to the smaller walls and the radical skaters happily manoeuvred around the amateurs. As I sat watching, I found it hard to reconcile the courteous kids at the skate park with the image of those vandalising louts that were talked about in council meetings. Had those residents never seen boys at play? Had none of them raised a boy? What did they expect the youth of their area to do after they grew out of swings and slippery dips? And didn't a wealthy council with a huge endowment of parks, beaches and bushland owe something to the boys of its area?

Every era constructs its image of children—whether it is their usefulness up chimneys, their dowry potential, their part in God's plan or their inheritance of the family business. Today is no different. Through media images, the social conversation, government policy, our interactions with children and memories of ourselves as children, we have built a modern image of children. The picture isn't flattering and it's a lot less flattering than the image parents have of their own children. We may know our 11-year-old to be a well-mannered skateboarder, but must accept that others will see him in the light cast by television news and their fearful imagination. We may accept our toddler with all the charms and challenges of that age group but other shoppers in the supermarket will only see the purple rage of a spoilt tot and the ineffectual discipline of a parent caught between a confectionary stand and a quick exit.

Each of us who decides to become a parent, has a picture of what our children might be but, overlaid on this, is the society's image of them. It doesn't take a lot of research or imagination to see that society's image of children today is one that is formed by media images, founded in the marketplace and fostered by fear. In theory, childhood may still be valued as a special space in a lifetime and considered a journey that is inherently worthwhile. In practice, it is more likely to be something budgeted for, negotiated around, managed, measured, monitored and, hopefully, expedited with the least amount of fuss. As Sheila Kitzinger says in *Ourselves as Mothers*:

Children are treated as a private indulgence. One consequence of this social attitude is that increasingly women approach birth and the initial tasks of motherhood in a business-like spirit, determined to do it well, but concerned to get back to the situation, in both their working and their private and social lives that existed before the baby was born. Employers, colleagues, friends and even a partner often expect this. It is 'returning to normal'.[1]

When the childless couple come to contemplate a future with children the conversation inevitably gets around to economic and management considerations. It's a rational way to enter the business of raising the next generation although, as we will see, if they heeded their rational minds, they would never proceed with the idea. The equation is simple, really. The costs of having children are mostly economic, the benefits are almost entirely psychological. The economic side of the equation has never been more prohibitive and the psychological side is getting tougher to imagine. Somewhere along the way most couples find that their emotions, dreams, egos and biology get the better of them and they take the plunge, despite the logic of the decision. Indeed, if it weren't for the power of love over logic, we'd be bulldozing empty suburbs annually.

According to a 2002 study on the cost of raising children, it takes $450 000 to raise two children to the age of twenty years. These calculations by the National Centre for Social Economic Modelling (NATSEM) found that two children cost just under a quarter of the average gross household income. Devoting a quarter of your gross income to the task of raising children is a big ask in a society that casts most options in life as 'lifestyle decisions'. But the bad news for those about to take the big step, is that the costs of children are loaded into the back end of the business not the front end. Most young couples do their sums on the basis of how much time they will take out of the workforce, what child care costs will do to their budget and how much they can spare for prams and jumpsuits. But babies are relatively cheap. It's teenagers who do the damage to household bottom lines. According to the NATSEM report, children under the age of five years cost $102 a week, while teenagers cost $318 and 18- to 24-year-olds cost $322 a week. The difference between baby wipes and acne treatments is even greater in higher-income households, where $458 a week is spent on teenagers and $466 on each child who has left school but lives at home. For low-income families, the teenager is a voracious consumer of cash. A child aged fifteen to 24 in a family that earns $567 a week, will consume 38 per cent of the family income. The trend of children living at home longer—half are still there at the age of 24 years—takes a toll on household budgets and retirement plans. If each of the two children stay at home for just one more year after the age of twenty, the lifetime cost of raising them goes from $450 000 to $482 000. The expression 'super siphons' has been coined for this generation of dependent adult children.

Obviously, the first child will have the biggest impact on household finances, but this survey indicates that the third child isn't as prohibitive as many might believe—costing half of what the first child did. On average, a family with one child will spend $183 a week, the two-child family devotes $310 a week to the kids and the three-child family $410 a week. The old saying that the third child raises itself owes something to financial data. 'It appears that by the time the third child arrives even high income families are feeling the pinch!' the report says.

When there is only one child, high-income couples spend much more than twice as much as low-income families, clearly indulging the new addition to their family ($281 a week vs. $111 a week). But by the time the third child arrives, high-income couples are spending less than twice as much on that child as low-income couples—$139 vs. $71 a week.[2]

Even women raised in middle-class families notice that the costs of raising children are higher than they were for their parents, or their grandparents. One school friend commented:

> As a young adult I had wanted five children, just like my mother and her mother before her. Despite this, finances do play a very large part. When your birthday present is a dozen nappies for the first baby and you can't work out how you will ever manage to feed and clothe it, you can't help but wonder why you are doing this. There is no way we could afford to have any more children and maybe we shouldn't have had any if costs were all we were thinking about.

These figures, while frightening in themselves, disguise the fact that more parents are footing costs they didn't face just a decade or two ago. The trend towards private education means that almost one-third of Australian children are sent to private schools. And the bills of private schooling are further inflated by the cost of boaters, books and keeping up appearances. The upkeep of teenagers may partly reflect the fact that toddlers raised in Target gear will turn around at the age of fourteen and insist that they must have the sort of sports shoes that gangs hijack kids for. Children, as we have seen, now stay at home longer and often without having to make contributions to their keep. Moreover, more children are going onto higher education and the cost of this has been outsourced—either to the family or to the child's future earnings. And, in capital cities, more parents are facing the quandary of financing their children into their own homes.

Some help them with home ownership, others subsidise their rents, but more of them simply house adult kids in the family home right through to their thirties.

The commitment to children doesn't stop at the wallet. It encompasses time, energy, mental and emotional support and great dollops of waiting, watching and wondering. If domestic work is the double shift, then emotional work must be the third shift. At the back of every mother's mind is an abacus that keeps track of the family's emotional wellbeing. I might be sitting here writing a book, but there is a mental counter that is forever being checked and updated. At the moment that checklist reads something like this:

Kate is looking peaky and tired. Three days to HSC trials. Must buy her a Nudie juice for brekkie and sushi for lunch and shut up about state of her room. Look for another King Lear source for her English. Would a 'queer theory' reading work? Must ring plumber today! Haven't seen Nicky for days. Wonder when she'll unpack her bag. Nag her about returning library book, get that $100 back from her. Remember to ask about Edwina. Tell Rog not to worry about her morning moods. Family not at best in morning. Maybe she has not come home because of the $100? Chicken must be used tonight. Boooorring. Use chorizo sausage this time. Keep eye on Toby's sore nose. Buy sausage when you pick him up at 5.35. And hair colour, eczema cream and mega vitamin B. Don't get hot chorizo, Kate will not eat it. Insist Toby does the public speaking course. Promise him something nice. Not money. Tell him that he can go out two nights a weekend. With girls. Has Rog given him The Talk?

The emotional shift isn't something that academic studies can measure but some have attempted to measure the time involved in raising children. Time-use studies conducted by Michael Bittman at the University of NSW give an idea of how much children take from our energy stores and our allotted hours. In a paper written with Lyn Craig, titled, 'The Time Costs of Children in Australia', Bittman and Craig found that the arrival of a child means that an extra four-and-a-half hours a day is needed just for the care of that child. This time cost decreases to three hours a day for a three- to four-year-old child and one-and-a-half hours a day for a primary school child. However, the psychic and physical costs of having children aren't shared equally. For a woman, the arrival of a child means she devotes three-and-a-half hours on top of her normal workload, whereas for a man, the arrival of that child only means an extra hour of work. And the sex segregation grows wider as the child ages. Women with preschool children do 75 per cent of the work involved with child care and women with primary-age children do 85 per cent of the child care. Women also miss out on sleep. This ranges between 36 minutes and 105 minutes, but men lose only between 20 minutes and 50 minutes a day. As the authors conclude, 'the consequence of the decision to become a mother is vastly different from the consequence of the decision to become a father'.[3]

The costs of raising children—both in time and money—are not just higher than ever, they have been privatised as never before. This has happened incrementally and often without parents realising it. Adding yet another cost related to having children is a little like feeding another mouth at the table—parents get used to the challenge of dividing a pie into smaller pieces. But most parents aren't so aware of how much they are contributing to the wealth of society today and tomorrow. Having children may be seen as a personal indulgence for parents but it is an economic imperative for society. Governments need children more than ever to support the growing army of elderly; employers need more of them to become the human capital of their HR-intensive businesses and society relies on a population of young who are well educated and socialised. Yet the cost of doing all this has increasingly been sheeted home to parents. This generation of parents are footing the bill for the economic and social prosperity of a nation and yet they are being treated as if they are indulging themselves by doing so.

The double whammy for parents is this: the costs of raising children have been privatised, yet the benefits of children have been socialised.

Children were once considered insurance for the future, for old age and infirmity. And they still are. Yet it's not insurance for their parents' old age—few of us expect our children to take us in, feed us tepid soup and tend our bed sores. But they are insurance for society. These children will grow up to be consumers, workers, taxpayers and aides in nursing homes and they're going to have to work at it harder than any other generation because there will be so few of them supporting so many aged. Parents are gifting their children to society and they are doing it at great cost to themselves.

The author of *The Empty Cradle*, Phillip Longman, put it succinctly in a piece he wrote for the *Washington Monthly* in 2004. Raising children is a 'sucker's game', he said.

> *The adults who sacrifice the most to create and mould this precious human capital, whether they be dutiful parents, daycare workers, school teachers, camp counsellors or even college professors, retain only a small share of the value they create. Indeed, as a rule, the more involved one becomes in the nurturing of the next generation, the less compensation one is likely to receive.*[4]

For many parents, especially those who had children later in life, this increased burden on their finances means they are stuck in the 24/7 workplace at an age when their parents were winding down. As the NATSEM survey showed, adult children are the most expensive and they are often still on the family payroll at a time when their parents are being turfed out of jobs or trying to save for retirement. Said one school friend:

> I feel that having kids later has benefits that we all know about—you can develop your career, enjoy the freedom of youth, become a more mature person and be financially more secure. On the flip side, you are more set in your ways, have less energy and time for them (especially if you have a career) and it also means that you have to keep working longer when you might wish to slow down or even retire. What has happened with several of my friends who are a little older is that they have ended up having to sell their homes and pull the kids out of private school to get by. In some instances (especially in the advertising industry where I have been working) once you reach 45 or 50, it's extremely hard to find work and the wives have had to find part-time work in retail which is all they can get at their age. This has happened to many people I know. They all had successful careers, did nothing wrong, just turned 50 and still had young children to support.

The privatisation of the costs of children has accelerated during the past few decades in the same way that so many community assets—transport, power, banks, telecommunications and education—have been privatised. It is part of the way that the capitalist system seeks to maximise profits from the society and defray its costs back onto society.

At its most obvious, this privatisation trend has led to the childcare industry being taken over by commercial groups, three of which have floated on the sharemarket. Companies like ABC Learning, Peppercorn Management Group and Hutchinson's Child

Care Services now operate hundreds of centres around Australia. Funded by government and parents, the private childcare centre now looks after shareholders as well as children.

But it's not just the capitalist economy of the past few decades that has shifted costs of children from the public sector to parental pockets. This movement is part of a much longer historical trend that has seen the image of children change from a social and economic asset—one that enhanced communities and provided security and wealth to parents—into an expensive parental hobby.

In his book, *Centuries of Childhood: A social history of family life*, Philippe Ariès pointed out that medieval society took responsibility for children from an early age. From the age of seven, children 'went into the great community of men, sharing in the work and play of their companions, old and young alike'. The family, Ariès wrote, 'fulfilled a function; it ensured the transmission of life, property and names; but it did not penetrate very far into human sensibility— realities such as the apprenticeship of children loosened the emotional bond between parents and children'. Given that none of us want a return to child labour, the picture that Ariès paints of the Middle Ages is one where children were considered a social asset; they were visible in society and their cost was underwritten by society from a very young age.

In European history, children began to be viewed more for themselves rather than just their utility when education was introduced in the seventeenth century. As Ariès noted:

> . . . this new concern about education would gradually install itself in the heart of society and transform it from top to bottom. The family ceased to be simply an institution for the transmission of a name and an estate—it assumed moral and spiritual functions, it moulded bodies

and souls. The care expended on children inspired new feelings, a new emotional attitude.[5]

Throughout the eighteenth century children could still be said to be 'the poor man's capital'. Even that iconic capitalist, Adam Smith, would refer to children as a source of opulence and prosperity to their parents. We wish.

In nineteenth-century Australia, children were still a light load on parents' time, responsibilities and pockets. In 1859, F. Fowler, a visiting Londoner, wrote of Sydney boys: 'Lazy as he is though, he is out in the world at ten years of age, earning good wages, and is a perfect little man, learned in all the ways and by-ways of life at twelve and thirteen'.[6]

The shift of children from the profit side of the ledger to the loss side occurred some time in the twentieth century, according to Bittman and Pixley's book, *The Double Life of the Family*.

The net flow of resources between children and parents had reversed in the 20th century from one where children brought in earnings and contributed labour to the household to one where parents must provide for their children over a long 'childhood'. There is also an opportunity cost in forgone earnings for the parent who cares for children. Hence, the decline in fertility is associated with 'the rise in price of human time', specifically a mother's, over the past two centuries.[7]

This cost hasn't just gone from society to families, it falls most heavily on women's resources. The authors point out that even as employers are making it tough for women to combine work with children, they are more dependent on what those women produce.

All elderly people (where pensions and superannuation are universal) are the free riders on this effort of bearing and raising children ... Employers are free riders in a rather different way. Not only do they want a supply of workers already 'endowed' with human capital due to the personal expenditure of the parents and government expenditure in education and training, but they also want an oversupply of this public good, so that inflation may be restrained and employers' prerogatives can be maintained. Employers want to free ride on the backs of mothers.

Not many women contemplate the idea of children with 'the rise in price of human time' in their mind. And yet, these fundamental inequities do percolate through to people's thinking. There is a profit and loss ledger in all our minds and, for the child-free person, it's awfully hard to balance the equation—especially as the cost side keeps getting bigger and the psychological side harder to imagine. They may be wise to the economic costs of children but it's more difficult to appreciate all the psychological benefits of children before the event.

People make their own calculations when they contemplate having a baby. The personal tally of costs is tough enough but it looks even tougher when and if they move beyond their own balance sheet and look at the economic commitment they are taking on for the benefit of society.

Policymakers and economists are happy to point out the inequities of raising children. An American economist, Shirley Burggraf, put it like this: 'People who never have children; parents who neglect, abuse or abandon children; deadbeat parents who don't pay child support, all have as much claim (in many cases more) on the earning of the next generation through the Social Security system as do the most dutiful parents.'[8]

Indeed, some socio-biologists believe we have inverted the principles of survival of the fittest. Instead of the most successful being those who survive to procreate, the most successful in our society are those who decide not to procreate. Those who survive the best in modern urban societies are those who can work the longest hours, who are mobile in employment and place, who can enjoy unencumbered leisure and consumption and yet still draw on the public purse for ill-health, defence, security and retirement. Those who are least equipped to survive are those who cannot work long hours, who carve out time for caring responsibilities, who share their leisure and consumption with dependents and divide their assets with the next generation. Perhaps there is some intuition of this among childless people or people who opt for a curtailed family life. Having children in a materialistic world is a suckers' game and the more you have to do with children, the less you'll be able to compete in the jungle of work and consumption.

Of course, few parents have children for economic reasons. Nor do they have children to improve the demographic profile of the next generation. They do it mostly for selfish reasons—all those warm, fuzzy, Hallmark card reasons. But many decide not to have children because of economic reasons or they delay the economic commitment of having children for so long that the question becomes rhetorical.

Researching the history of children from economic necessity to emotional indulgence, another social picture of children emerges. Children were once in society, as Ariès says. From the age of seven, children worked and played alongside adults in 'the great community of men'. Even babies and toddlers were in the picture as mothers brought them along for the day's work. That classic Brueghel painting of sixteenth-century European village life, shows children of all ages playing in the town square and participating in the activities of the town. The presence of children in society is also apparent right through to the 1970s—whether they are historical photos of street urchins in nineteenth-century cities or the 1950s scenes of billy carts careening down suburban streets or 15-year-old apprentices going off to work at BHP in the 1970s. Sometime in the last few decades, however, children began disappearing from view. Take a Brueghel-like photo of the town square today and you'll see men and women scurrying to and fro the workplace; you'll see couriers, shoppers, joggers, tourists and aged visitors but rarely a child. Those hurly-burly images of mothers with children hanging off the pram, children travelling in packs, families en route or even teenagers in trysts are missing.

It's not just cradles that are emptying. Our public spaces are emptying of children and when we don't have children in our faces, in our streets and in our daily lives, the public psyche loses sight of children. Once they're out of sight, they're out of mind. We are more likely to forget about the needs of children, the joys of children and the nature of children and many more are likely to forget to have children. One of the boasts in Ethan Watters' *Urban Tribes* was the claim that for his gang of singles living in fashionable parts of San Francisco, it was possible to go for days without seeing a child.

Where have the children gone? The short answer is to institutions. More babies and toddlers are in childcare centres or in homes being looked after by family day carers, nannies and grandparents. The primary school children are either in school, in after-school care or being ferried to one of their many after-school activities. Secondary school children are also in school, at the library or being ferried home for study, tutoring or onto another extra-curricular activity, or doing part-time jobs. It's difficult to see what's not there, but sometimes it becomes apparent what's happening behind the closed doors of childhood. In 2004, politicians and community leaders were getting concerned about the skyrocketing rates of childhood obesity. Inquiries and reports were commissioned to discover why children were growing so fat and one of the key findings was that more children were coming home after school to empty houses and spending the afternoon in front of the television with an array of snacks. Those children who had disappeared from the streets were emerging into adulthood fat and unfit, much to the surprise and ire of society.

Childhood has been institutionalised and managerialised—and if that's beginning to sound like the workplace, it's not so surprising. We have built childhood around the image of the workplace. Children's hours are timetabled with the precision of the clock-on/clock-off workplace; their outcomes—health, literacy, crime—are measured with the tools of management; their costs have been privatised and the care of them has been outsourced—from nappy services, to child care, tutoring and entertaining.

The speed of our working lives sets the pace for our children's lives. I remember taking my two young girls to the local pool one weekend. I was in a rush. The weekly shopping still had to be done, the house was a wreck, we were going out later and I figured we had 45 minutes max to spend at the pool. As she was struggling into her cossie, three-year-old Kate asked, 'Mum, why do we dash all the time?' It wasn't said in anger or frustration, it was more idle curiosity. 'Let's dash' was something I said to them several times a day. Going out, coming home, getting ready, I was always saying, 'Come on, let's dash'. I looked at Kate trying to hurry the process of getting into her cossie and wondered what I was doing to her childhood. There was an old sign in the pool changing room that said No Loitering. Not a chance, I thought as I shepherded the girls to the pool.

The institutions of childhood are indeed beginning to resemble workplaces. The creation of childcare centres has been central to women's ability to move out into the world of work. Women no longer have to argue about whether they should have child care—that debate was won in the 1980s—but they are still bearing too much of the cost of this care and often they struggle to find the sort of care that fits in with their needs. But what is overlooked in all the talk about child care is how it has changed perceptions of children and, in particular, ideas about how children should fit into society.

The debate about child care, especially involving babies, is always an emotional one—not just because it divides conservative and liberal ideas of the family but because the practice of placing babies in long periods of institutional care is still being evaluated. One of the most controversial cartoons done by Michael Leunig was his 1995 one, captioned 'Thoughts of a Baby Lying in a Child Care Centre'.[9] Leunig said he was motivated by the question: 'What does a child feel when the mother is suddenly not there—the breast, the nipple, its whole world is taken away?' In a *Sydney Morning Herald* interview he added,

> The mother/baby relationship is a very particular one; it lies at the heart of our culture and I think we're losing this vital relationship. We've become ignorant about the psychological and emotional state of the infant, in the same way we were about Aborigines when we used to take their children away—as if they didn't have the same feelings as us. It's become an expectation that when you have a child you put it in a creche and go back to work. No one is questioning that expectation.[10]

The cartoon hit a nerve. An *Age* columnist, Moira Rayner, said: 'Depending on which letters to the editor you read, he is either St Michael, Defender of the Innocent or Michael the misogynist . . . I think of him fondly as a slightly daffy hitch-hiker on an alien starship whose crew is on crack.'[11]

The baby in the childcare cradle from dawn to dusk is still a rarity. According to Australian Bureau of Statistics figures, almost half the children under the age of five spend some time in formal child care, but only 7 per cent of babies less than a year old are in formal care, whereas three-quarters of three- and four-year-olds are in some form of care. And extended hours in care are less common than they were. In 1993, 12 per cent of children in formal care were in centres for more than 30 hours a week, but by 2002 this had fallen to 9 per cent. On both a personal and societal level, we obviously still have misgivings about leaving babies in extended care.

These misgivings were compounded in 2002 when Melbourne University education academic Kay Margetts released a study showing the social, behavioural and educational impact of various forms of child care. She concluded that children who spent more than 30 hours a week in child care in their first few years had lower social skills, more problem behaviours and performed worse academically. She also found that children who were looked after by grandparents in their early years had worse academic performances, especially if the care was for more than 30 hours a week. Moreover, while mother care augured well for most outcomes, intensive mother care in the year before school, especially if it was for five or more days a week, was associated with sad, lonely and anxious children. The best outcome for children was a mixture of care—mother care, especially in the first two years, with child care.[12] The mixed approach to child care was better than both intensive forms of institutional care or exclusive mother care. But perhaps not better for the workplace.

The idea that we have structured child care too much around the demands of the workplace rather than around the best interests of the child is one that is shared by Careen Leslie, director of the Wiradjuri Centre and early childhood course convenor at the University of Canberra. This centre is used as a research centre by the university and Leslie is obviously aware of the best practices in child care. Yet, its director has reservations about intensive use of childcare centres. In an interview for this book she said:

> We have structured care about the needs of the workforce but it doesn't suit small children to be in care from early morning to early evening most days of the week. You wouldn't want to work that long, so how can you expect children to like it? This pressure is going to grow now that we have 24 hour centres and private companies running centres because they are interested in getting children for the longest period possible.

She adds that childcare centres are licensed to provide one carer for five babies whereas if a woman had quintuplets, she'd be eligible for government assistance—and, no doubt, a spread in the *Australian Women's Weekly*. Mothers, she says, won the right to work but only on men's terms. So not only do mothers have to work on men's terms, their children do too. Parents who want to maintain a commitment to careers have no choice but to outsource the care of children and, with the lengthening of the working day, children's days in care grow longer.

Child care is a crucial support for both mothers and fathers in the workforce but the outsourcing of care for children has different impacts on the relationship between parents and children. In the best outcomes, it gives parents a break from the 24/7 responsibility of caring for children and makes the time they spend together more treasured experiences and often more fun-based than duty-bound. But at the other extreme it can remove parents from the nurturing role and the bonds of intimacy that come with caring. Careen Leslie fears we are becoming remote from our caring roles.

Nobody wants to deal with children, they don't want to touch them, they don't want to wipe their noses or do any of that hands-on business. Women didn't want to do it day and night, as Betty Friedan pointed out, and men refused to take it up, so that duty has been transferred to childcare centres. But not even childcare workers want to do it, when graduates of early childhood studies decide where they'll work, they invariably end up working in primary schools because this end of the business is too hard and undervalued. We're not a child-friendly society and we're becoming more unfriendly. We may say we like children but we have very little tolerance of them and the less we have to do with them, the less capable and interested we are in them.[13]

The crisis in caring crops up throughout the roles that have traditionally been in women's hands. Mothers are no longer going to do the endless shift at home alone with the children, childcare workers are leaving the caring industry, nurses have been in short supply in Australia (and many other countries) for a decade and the teaching profession is chronically short of people. The caring professions are treated like voluntary work—noble but not worth a proper wage. Women, who once dominated these professions, are less likely to stay with such low pay rates and are no longer content to be society's carers and nurturers when those roles have been so devalued.

The heat in this issue of who cares for children is obviously still smouldering. But the separation of young children from the public realm is just the beginning of the disappearance of all children from society. During the years of primary schooling, children are removed from the streets, parks, workplaces and homes, partly so they can be looked after to allow parents to work but also for their own protection. During the secondary years, they disappear into study and after-school sports, partly for their own development but also to keep them out of trouble. For many people, the sight of teenagers in 'gangs' is a frightening experience—even if they are only skateboarding, gossiping or making for the mall. As Penelope Leach says in *Children First*, we have removed children from the adult world where they once watched, helped and emulated and we've placed them instead in a series of 'special environments' designed to keep them out of harm's way and adults' way.

In so far as parents' stressful dilemmas are recognised at all, the socially approved mechanisms for coping with them do not aim for greater integration of children but for increasing separation from them; separation of personal and domestic commitments from work commitments and therefore of children's lives from adults' lives.[14]

The idea that we have constructed childhood around the needs of the marketplace is probably not a comfortable one. Many believe we left our mercantile ideas of childhood—the kiddies down the mines and up the chimneys—back in the days of Dickens. And yet much of our public discussion of children and, indeed, public policy revolves around the outcomes of childhood not the experiences of children. Trawl through newspaper files on children and you'll find scores of stories on childhood obesity, behavioural problems, illnesses, buying habits, school achievements and, of course, the cost of them, but you'll rarely encounter stories on the experiences of being a child. Whether it is news reports on childhood or projections of childhood in our entertainment media, children are getting down to business, more or less successfully.

This construction of childhood is different from the childhoods experienced by most adults—especially older adults. Memories of childhood in the 40s, 50s, 60s and 70s revolve around unfettered time, extended leisure, endless summer holidays, afternoons spent mucking about on quiet streets and weekends spent roaming around the neighbourhood. But, more interestingly, the structured, institutional nature of childhood today is a sharp contrast to the fun, silliness and endless moments of trivia that are now associated with the lives of childless adults. While the early years of life are spent in institutions, with structured time and measurable outcomes, the reproductive years are increasingly spent around cafes and Fooz ball tables among friends who are having the time of their life while thinking they have all the time in the world.

We haven't made the life of children very attractive either for them or for those who might be thinking of having one. What do childless couples think when they try to imagine a life with children? They might envisage Bart Simpson; they might remember the toddler they saw at the supermarket. They might remember the conversation with the parents who pay $350 in after-tax money to a childcare centre or the older parent who can't afford to retire. And, against these social images of children, they'll try to imagine the child of their future, that pudgy baby that has lain dormant in their imagination. They might try to imagine their work identities morphing into parental ones; their home being taken over by Lego; their characters being expanded by a new role in life, their future being drawn in the sand of humanity. Or they might not even think about it. At the very least, the removal of children from the social sphere makes it easy to forget to have children. But it also makes it more difficult for us to live with children because we forget what they are and how they behave; we forget how to wipe their noses, how to play with them and how to talk to them. Eventually what we don't know, we either forget or fear. As Careen Leslie says,

> Children are more remote from society than ever. They're meant to be looked after somewhere else—somewhere outside of the home,

somewhere other than work and you certainly don't want to encounter them on the street. You go to work and you wouldn't know whether people have children or not. You can go days without seeing children in some areas and that's seen as desirable.[15]

This forgetting of childhood is part of the human condition. As Randall Jarrell wrote in the introduction to Christina Stead's *The Man Who Loved Children*, 'One of the most obvious facts about grown-ups, to a child, is that they have forgotten what it is like to be a child'.[16] But that forgetting is made greater by the lack of children in public life today—partly because there are fewer of them and partly because they have been isolated from the world of adults. If you only run into a child a few times a week, it's easy to forget to have one. And if you see more youths throwing rocks on the television set than playing in public, then you're likely to be frightened by the idea of boys gathering together to play in a skate park.

Myths, lies and masks

My young sister is in labour. It is an early stage of labour. She's been in the birthing room for several hours and is fast running out of patience. I am there to offer a cool washer, gratuitous advice and the opportunity for her to be vile to me without my extracting revenge. After another stupendous contraction, she turns to me with wild eyes and fixes me with a question: 'Tell me it doesn't get any worse than this.' She's asking me because she thinks I'll tell her the truth. I am supposed to be her advocate for drugs, her pinching post and her third opinion, so she expects honesty. What can you say? 'Of course, it gets harder! You ain't seen nothing yet. The pain you are about to enter will transport you out of your mind and into a place that is all body, all animal. You will be possessed by pain and purpose in a way you never believed possible, even now as you struggle with contractions that pound your body like tsunamis. Soon, you will barely be able to surface for breath.' Perhaps not. So, do you tell her a lie? Do you tell her it will be over soon, that the worst has passed and so rob her of the chance to garner up new sources of energy and power? And then, when it does get worse, leave her feeling conned by those who offer cool washers and cruel promises.

What do you tell women who are about to become mothers? Whether they are hours away from holding their first child or months away from taking the plunge into pregnancy or years away from considering the prospect of parenthood, is it possible to describe what it's like? Is it wise to tell them? Is it even realistic for one mother's experience to be passed onto another woman as the archetypal experience? The quandary I faced in that birthing room is similar to the sort of problems faced by mothers who attempt to tell childless women what motherhood is like.

It seems perverse that in an era of information, when there is so much literature on parenting, child-raising and ways of combining work with family, that the first thing many new mothers say is: 'Why didn't they tell me it was going to be like this?' The language barrier between women who've had children and those who haven't has become such a talking point that it has earned its own genre on the bookshelves. If you search Barnes and Noble for books on motherhood, many of the 4182 titles that crop up are about the lies, myths, shocks and misconceptions of motherhood and those are the ones that end up on bestseller lists. Some of the better known ones are: *The Myths of Motherhood*, *The Cultural Contradictions of Motherhood*, *The Mask of Motherhood*, *Misconceptions*, *The Price of Motherhood*, *The Mommy Myth*, *The Hidden Feelings of Motherhood* and *Mother Shock*. There's a clue somewhere in there about the reality of motherhood. Just for curiosity's sake, ask Google to find references on the 'facts of motherhood' and then ask it to track down stuff on the 'lies of motherhood'. References to the facts of motherhood—73 600—only just outnumber references to the lies of motherhood—61 400.

The literature that tackles the lies, myths and misconceptions of motherhood attempts to bridge the gap between the expectations of modern women and the realities of modern motherhood—one being more modern than the other. Many try to peel back the discontent of mothers and find out why. Other authors explore their own experiences and ask, How come? Most try to answer the sort of questions that women ask before maternity without resorting to the sort of smug replies that some mothers give them.

There are many statements that women and men make when they decide to have a baby. Here are some common ones:

I'm going to have a natural birth.

This was a big one among my friends and is still common among those who do yoga, read Sheila Kitzinger and don't have too many girlfriends who've had kids. The statement presumes that martial arts, diligent reading and a sense of control will get them through birth.

I'll get back to normal in no time.

This is a favourite of those who've used pregnancy as an excuse to get stuck into Krispy Kremes. It's reinforced by employers, partners and obstetricians. And they're probably right about abdominal muscles and sleeping patterns, but this statement presumes there is something intrinsically good about where you've come from.

We're going to share the child-raising.

Women say this while their partners sit there and nod. It is possible. After all, people have climbed Mount Everest and walked on the moon. However, the majority of women—even feminist author Naomi Wolf—find themselves drifting back into traditional gender roles. Why is it so?

We don't want it to affect our relationship.

Men and women both say this, especially men who've heard about the dearth of sex after birth. Once again, it presumes that the relationship is perfect or that the baby will only change it for the worse.

The baby will fit into our life.

If you're a field worker in a developing country, your baby can be slung around the torso in a baby carrier where it can root for the nipple and suckle all day while you thrash grains. If not . . .

My workplace is child-friendly.

Women who've only read the company mission statement on the Internet might be in for a surprise. Ditto the women whose boss has made a vague comment about loving children while asking what date—exactly—she was returning to work. Those who've searched out mothers in their workplace will be better informed.

All childcare centres are good these days.

Yep, we monitor the operations of all childcare centres just like we check the hygiene standards of restaurants, the police record of teachers and the safety compliance of cars being registered.

I'm going to love being a full-time mother.

Often said in high-rise offices late at night by women who can see suburbia twinkling in the distance and imagine that somewhere out there are a lot of relaxed mothers, who drink coffee of a morning, play tennis of an afternoon and cart charming children along for the ride.

I'm afraid of turning into my mother.

Such a common one that the word 'matraphobia' was invented to express the fear of reliving your mother's life. Unfortunately each generation has a good reason for this fear.

We want a big family.

A big family these days is often three to four children. If you start at twenty or 25 years, there's a good chance of achieving this. If you start at the age of 30, the chances are much slimmer, 35 and you might have to settle for a litter of Labradors.

These questions often reflect the fact that many women approaching pregnancy and childbirth haven't been around children for a long time. The concerns of the soon-to-be mothers are also rooted in their own worldview. They reflect the sort of issues that occupy women who are engaged in their working lives, living independent lifestyles and competing against men on a fairly level field. Women in their late twenties and thirties are used to controlling their own destiny, writing their own script and making decisions on behalf of themselves and their partners. But the questions asked by women approaching maternity aren't resolved by the sort of advice offered by mothers. The headline statements by mothers to childless women include:

Children change everything.

This is often said by a mother who is wondering where her bladder control went, why her husband is never home before 8 p.m., how her hair went curly and why her boss puts her at the bottom of the 'cc' list on emails.

You learn to live with chaos.

This is the new mother's response to a surprise visit from a single girlfriend as she ushers her friend past the unmade beds, the field of Lego in the lounge room and into the kitchen where unwashed bottles compete for sink space with takeaway containers.

You don't know love till you've had a child.

A popular mantra at mothers' coffee mornings but not so welcome when you mention it to the globetrotting girlfriend whose seven-year relationship with a gorgeous 43-year-old executive has just ended because he thinks he's too young for children.

Children teach you how to live unselfishly.

Mothers write this in emails to far-flung girlfriends after they have finished the burnt chop, read the home reader to the five-year-old, breast-fed the baby and opened a cleanskin wine from the cellar while waiting for their husbands, who are unselfishly earning extra money in overtime.

You'll learn what it means to be tired.

See above.

You become fully human as a parent.

The mother reminds herself to tell her friends this when she sees them next because at the moment she can feel every bone in her body, her fight-or-flight responses are on alert and she growls like a Neanderthal as she passes the playroom.

You are investing in the future with children.

The mother has just been in a protest for more childcare places; she is thinking of switching her vote to the nice man who reads to children and knows she should feel guilty about what the disposable nappies are doing to the environment. She's trying not to think of her superannuation savings.

The talk that goes on between women with children and childless women could hardly be called a conversation. It's more like a game of charades in which neither party is interested in winning. Aside from the fact that those refrains heard from mothers aren't very useful, there is a smugness that underlines much of the mother rhetoric. The UK-based columnist, Zoe Williams, referred to this as 'the cult of parenthood' in a piece published in the *Good Weekend* magazine in 2004. 'Modern parents are engaged in a ceaseless attempt to appropriate all human experience, from tiredness to spirituality, as theirs and theirs alone', she wrote. 'If we are to accept this as truth, then non-mothers exist in a kind of cognitive half-light, and we are inchoate and immature.'[1]

There have been waves of tension between women without children and mothers throughout the last few decades; there have been episodes of verbal warfare between working mothers and stay-at-home mothers and there are daily skirmishes between mothers and fathers over the carve-up of parental responsibilities. But maybe much of this frustration is being misdirected. Childless women who are critical of mothers may well be expressing a frustration that their choices aren't supported; that their choices weren't really choices; or that they are still trying to find meaning for a path they may not have chosen. In lashing out at the inequities of their lives as mothers, women tend to pick on the unfortunate soul who's just walked into the kitchen, or the old girlfriend who she thinks doesn't understand her plight. Fathers often find themselves caught between a demanding workplace and an overwhelmed home base; between old role models and new expectations and they rarely time their entrance into the kitchen well. Not many of them look at the systems they are operating under to see the invisible hands working.

The communication barrier between women who are on different sides of that pink line of the pregnancy test isn't as big a problem as the difference between women's own expectations and the reality they subsequently encounter. And much of this dissonance lies in the fact that women's lives as independent, childless people have changed radically in the past generation while the roles of parenting have remained rooted in a different era.

Two generations ago, women in the developed world had little time between leaving their birth families and starting their own families. Most women spent only a few years outside of families and their expectations of even this short period away from family were often limited to finishing their education or getting a 'little' job to fill in time. If they had dreams of careers, travel or independence then, as Betty Friedan pointed out, these mostly remained in the realm of fantasy or in the lives of the unmarried women. The shock of motherhood, for previous generations, was tempered by their recent experience of being in a family and the fact that most felt they had no choice in the matter. And, even when they were taken aback by the adjustments needed, it wasn't acceptable to talk publicly about feeling estranged from something that was supposed to be natural.

Contrast that generation's experiences with those of women today. Most come from smaller families and so, by the time they have their first child at the age of 30, they wouldn't have lived with a young child for 25 to 30 years. Even though they stay in the family home for longer, they live there as relatively carefree adults in mostly adult households. The mantra for modern women is self-development—develop your career, your fitness and the self. And the subtext of that mantra is control—modern women are imbued with the idea that they can control their career, their finances, their relationships and their abdominal muscles. By the time she arrives at the door of pregnancy, modern woman is full of confidence, competencies and questions. And she doesn't realise she's knocking on the door of a different country.

The role of motherhood and, more generally, family is mired in the past. Arlie Hochschild referred to it in her 1989 book, *The Second Shift*, as 'the stalled revolution'. Peggy Orenstein in *Flux* calls it a 'half-changed' world and Barbara Pocock in the *Work/Life Collision* refers to the 'unrenovated models of motherhood and fatherhood'. What they all refer to is the revolution that *hasn't* happened in the home.

The family home is a place of myths, lies and misconceptions. It is a place where many strive to be equal but few are. As I remarked above, even Naomi Wolf found the family wasn't the sort of place she expected. As she writes in *Misconceptions*:

> When I was growing up, I knew exactly how I wanted my life to be 'after the revolution' in gender roles and work expectations that I fully expected would arrive just in time—that is, before I had children. I had wanted to work at a job I cared about and share child-rearing with a man I loved. I had wanted a mother and a father raising children side by side, the man moving into the world of children, the women into the world of work, in equitable balance . . . 'Ha', as women usually comment at this point in the fantasy.[2]

Another feminist, Harriet Lerner, who wrote *The Mother Dance*, was also shocked at how quickly her marriage defaulted to gender roles.

I felt as if an invisible force field had pushed Steve back into his previously normal life, while I was being pushed in the opposite direction. The force field was everywhere—in the structure and policies of our work system, in the unspoken attitudes of colleagues, in the cultural traditions over generations, in the roles and rules of the families we came from, in the outposts in our heads, and in the very air we breathed.[3]

The myths of the hearth have bred academic expressions such a 'pseudo mutuality', where a man underestimates a woman's contribution to the household while over-estimating his contribution, and 'cultural cover-up', where women allow men to get away with pseudo mutuality because they want to maintain peace. Women's shame, surprise or simple bewilderment at the fact that their lives are devolving to family models they've only witnessed on repeats of 60s sit coms keeps many quiet. The modern, childless woman, presumes as Naomi Wolf did, that the home has undergone the same sort of revolution that swept through the workplace, economics, gender relations and global relations. And, if they do suspect what really goes on in most families after baby comes home, they swear it's not going to happen to them. But rhetoric doesn't make for a revolution and many of those women who enter pregnancy with a list of what they're going to do and not do will find themselves a few years later giving sage—sometimes smug-sounding—advice to women who don't know what it's going to be like.

There is now a whole shelf load of literature that attempts to open the window on modern mothering, but not too long ago there weren't so many words for these misconceptions. Susan Maushart's

The Mask of Motherhood was one of the first books to address it in Australia when it came out in 1997. As she says, 'Most women in our society—particularly those who are middle-class, white and educated—are still in the closet on the subject of motherhood. And "faking it" in our public behaviour and public discourse has become a way of life'.4 In those few decades from the start of modern liberation to the more honest discussion of the reality of motherhood, there was something of a conspiracy of silence among women. This silence was born of fear and nurtured by embarrass-ment. Women who felt as if they were on probation working in a man's world didn't want to discuss how tough it was doing both men's work and women's work. And if they didn't discuss it with other working mothers, it was probably because they presumed that everyone else could cope just fine, that all those other women were the superwomen she read about. And if a new mother came up to her at work and confided that she Didn't Know It Was Going to Be Like This, then maybe she felt a little Schadenfreude. But the public discussion is under way. The myths, lies and misconceptions now have book titles, television shows and radio talk-back sessions devoted to them. We shouldn't be as surprised about the other world as we were in the past.

But perhaps there is no way a person can adequately prepare for the transition to motherhood. You can put out signposts but you can't foretell the journey. American feminist Gloria Steinem alluded to this in a powerful way. In a quote that crops up throughout literature on motherhood she said: 'Perhaps we share stories in much the same spirit that explorers share maps, hoping to speed each other's journey, but knowing the journey we make will be our own.'

When I was pregnant with my first child I had the list of do's and don'ts—it was a long list. I heard some stories from colleagues who'd had kids—people who weren't like me. I even went along to a mothers' coffee hour, where I held a few babies, talked diapers—and swore I'd never be like that. I read books on birthing and I was right there with Sheila Kitzinger enjoying the moment—or rather, enjoying her moment, mine was yet to come. I had a child-friendly workplace—even though the personnel manager said he'd never had to process a maternity leave application before. And yet the reality was . . . different. When I reflect on how unprepared I was for reality, I sometimes think that I didn't ask enough questions about the deeper, metaphysical aspects of mothering. You know, what it feels like to be so besotted with a baby that you crane to take a peek at her in the rear vision mirror every time the car stops and sometimes when you're still driving. What it feels like when the touch of a child is too much, when you can't take any more demands on your body and you can't take in any more information and you just want to have your body, mind and soul back for a few unadulterated minutes of being you. Or how the fact that you want to do the best thing by your child means that you are finally going to have to learn to control your temper, learn some patience and finish the growing-up that you never quite completed in adolescence. At other times, I think I should have asked more basic questions and not just said to my post-partum girlfriends, 'But what do you *do* all day?' Maybe, I didn't have the patience to listen when I was a career woman in control of her destiny. All I know is that the questions I asked on an intellectual level—or rational level—didn't prepare me for much.

Nowadays I think that if mothers' answers are inadequate, it might be because the questions aren't the right ones. The questions of childless women are formed in a society of timetables, control, independence and the pursuit of happiness, serenity and self-fulfilment. The answers from mothers come from a place of 'chaos, complexity, turbulence and truth', as Harriet Lerner put it in *The Mother Dance*. 'Kids,' she added, 'are the best teachers of life's most profound spiritual lessons; that pain and suffering are as much a part of life as happiness and joy; that change and impermanence are all we can count on for sure; that we don't really run the show; and that if we can't find the maturity to surrender to these difficult truths, we'll always be unhappy that our lives—and our children's—aren't turning out the way we expected.'⁵ Come in, Zoe Williams.

In some ways, I think preparing people for parenthood is a little like giving kids sex education. Kids come along to PD sessions with the vague hope that they're going to learn the practicalities of romance. They want to know whether you should ask for a kiss or just do it; and how you get around braces and noses and then move on to other interesting areas in one smooth motion. They want to know how two bodies negotiate their way around each other and into that moment of bliss. And the sex education teacher tells them how all these weird little sperm come out of the diagram of a penis and go up the diagram of a uterus, wiggle around like an ADD kid until one of them scores with this big fat egg. One is a lesson in biology, the other is a desire for dating information. Neither of them say too much about sex.

This coyness to speak on either the mundane level of motherhood or the metaphysical level is reminiscent of the ways our society once talked about sex. The subject of sex was once textbook stuff, talked about more in theory than reality. That was before *The Joy of Sex, The Hite Report, Fear of Flying, Sex and the City*, the explicit chatter of reality shows and Internet pornography. Sex may no longer be a rude shock for the young virgin on her honeymoon but motherhood appears to have taken its place.

Of course, the genre of motherhood myths—some call it whinge lit—impacts on women's decision to have children. The realists may decide that if their sisters haven't been able to sort out a better way to be a mother, then they're not going to open that door. Even when they hear the positive stories of the life-changing nature of being a mother, the simple joys of watching a baby sleep or hearing a dawn song from a toddler, they sometimes react like Zoe Williams did— reject it as a club of the boring and sanctimonious. But the impact of the double talk on motherhood isn't just on women's decision to remain childless. There is statistically a greater impact on national birth rates by women who decide to downsize their family ambitions. That is, women who experience a big discrepancy between what they thought motherhood would be and what it turned out to be, will sometimes decide not to have another child. The growing prevalence of the one-child family has been associated with many contributing factors—relationship break-ups, late start to child-bearing and the demands of careers—but a crucial element is women's experience of that first child in the home. According to the preliminary results from the study done at Brown University in the United States (referred to in chapter four), the relationship between unequal domestic lives and low fertility is a powerful one.[6] For the modern woman the shock of returning to an unrenovated domestic scene with the new baby can be greater than the pain of the birth or the relentless rhythms of a newborn. This space shouldn't still belong just to her! Why hasn't it changed? Does every woman find this or is there something I haven't figured out yet? Did someone forget to tell me something? The same questions are asked year after year in countries around the world and the answers are just as hard to find.

When I emerged from the hospital after my sister's baby boy had been born, I remembered how I felt after I left hospital with my first baby. I looked at the women in the street with prams or toddlers and thought, 'You're a hero, you're all heroes'. I wanted to shake their hands and tell them how amazing it was that they'd been through birth. I also vaguely wondered why women didn't shout about their accomplishment more often, why these daily feats of endurance weren't celebrated the same way that mountain climbing and marathon running were. And, yes, I felt silly thinking these things but what was even sillier was that at the time I didn't stop to think that if birth was such an amazing secret to me, what else was in store for me?

Post-script: What did I say to my sister? Words to the effect that the pain would get more powerful but it would be more constructive, she'd be able to work with it. Just words, they didn't make things easier but, at least, they didn't make things worse. And she didn't slug me for saying them.

No dogs, no children

In Margaret Atwood's *The Handmaid's Tale*, women have become prisoners of their biology. In a declining society, breeders like Offred have one function—to produce children. 'Think of it as being in the army', Aunt Lydia tells Offred, who sits all day in a white cell beneath a pretty print of blue irises.[1]

Both my daughters have read *The Handmaid's Tale* as a school text so I asked them what they thought of it. In particular, I wanted their response to the idea that in a society desperately in need of children, fertile women will lose their freedom to become handmaids of procreation. Both liked the book for different reasons. Kate liked it because it was fantasy; Nicole liked it because it was so realistic. Hello?

In her history of the Middle Ages, *A Distant Mirror*, Barbara Tuchman speculates that the devastation of the Black Death in the fourteenth century might have led Europe into the Renaissance. The plagues, which halved the population of Europe, unseated old ways, beliefs and power bases. As she writes, 'Once people envisioned the possibility of change in a fixed order, the end of an age of submission came in sight; the turn to individual conscience lay ahead. To that extent the Black Death may have been the unrecognised beginning of modern man.'[2]

History and fiction give different impressions of what happens after populations have been decimated. In history's version, society is liberated from old ways. In fiction's version, society closes down. To readers of the lie of the land, today's society could go either way—into historical revival or a bleak future. One reader might look at what we've done to motherhood, the family, communities and populations and decide that the future looks a lot like Offred's world. Another reader might read the same information and believe that Offred's world could never happen here, that future societies will realise they have to improve the lot of women and families. A Renaissance of family or Offred's World?

There are many ways in which the world is being remade in the wake of dramatic demographic changes. Much of this change is at a glacial pace so it's hard to spot, but there are already shifts in attitudes and practices that are going to have far-reaching implications. Emerging attitudes to reproductive biology, the embrace of the single life, the difficulty of reconciling work with family life, are all determining the shape of the future. All those trends that have impacted on decisions to have children will continue to ricochet into the future. And they might be hard to reverse. Demographic trends are tough ships to turn about. One of the most worrying emerging trends in demography is how the disappearance of children is affecting the decisions that young people make about their future family. Child-scarce generations tend to breed child-unfriendly futures.

As large parts of the world wind down their future populations, there are emerging signs as to how modern society will respond to the emptying playgrounds and, according to demographer Peter McDonald, the signposts aren't encouraging.

As you get more and more people who don't have children, society adjusts to that and it becomes more attractive not to have children. Having fewer children doesn't usually mean you treasure the children you have, it generally means the opposite. Germany, for instance, is emerging as a no-child preference country. German demographers are talking about 30 per cent or more of German women not having a child and they say this is the result of a very child unfriendly society.[3]

Germany is an outpost of the low-fertility frontier. It was the first European country to experience below-replacement fertility—it was below 2.1 by the late 1960s—and so it has spent more than a generation with fewer prams on the streets, with schools emptying and singles bars booming. At the same time, the better life expectancy and early retirement trends have swelled the ranks of retirees filling spa towns. Children are not quite a memory but they are increasingly remote from many Germans' lives and Germans are deciding they quite like that.

In a report based on the Eurobarometer 2001 survey, demographers found that for the first time in history, people's desire for families has fallen below the replacement level—that is, the ideal family size for young men and women in German-speaking countries has fallen from two to 1.7. They don't just fail to have enough children to replace themselves; they start off their adult lives not wanting that many children. The report, *The Decline of Family Size Preferences in Europe: Towards sub-replacement levels?*, said the findings in German-speaking countries will shift the debate about fertility. To date, birth rates have declined despite the fact that most people still want two children or, in some countries, three or four children. So, much of the policy work has been based on helping people achieve their dreams for a family. In many ways, national governments have recognised that it is a basic human right to have children and it is a fundamental duty of government to help people achieve this human right. Now, for the first time, people are saying they don't want children—at least not enough to replace themselves. So what do governments do when their people no longer want children? Do they try to reignite their family ambitions or do they recognise a new reality and take family off the national agenda?

According to the report authors, Joshua Goldstein, Wolfgang Lutz and Maria Rita Testa, these diminished family ambitions among Germans 'have emerged as a natural consequence of a history of low fertility . . . more broadly, it may be that a culture of low fertility has emerged'. The implications for German-speaking countries are not just further falls in the fertility level—it stands at 1.5—but more dramatic implications for the whole of the low-fertility world. For Germany, it is likely to lead to what demographers refer to as a spiralling down of future populations—fewer people want fewer children and end up having even fewer children than expected so there are fewer people in the next generation who may want even fewer children . . . But the broader implications are that people of the rest of Europe—and other parts of the world—will follow in the footsteps of Germany and decide that they too don't want family in their lives. As the authors say, the results 'indicate a deeper and more durable societal change, a decline in family size ideals . . . for the first time people's stated preferences have deviated from the two-child ideal that has held such sway since the baby boom.'[4]

While the four-child family was the image of the 50s—and reality for many—the idea of the two-child family has been entrenched in modern society since effective contraception gave people control over how many children they had. The two-child ideal was partly borne out of worries about the population explosion in the early 70s, but it has since been held as something of a sacred idea. You have one for the father and one for the mother. Some have believed it is hard-wired into us to replace ourselves; that women will instinctively opt for two children; that biology will generally ensure the future of humanity. This can no longer be taken for granted. There are more and more indications that family size is, as they say, a social construct: that the ideal family is not something written into our biology, but something that is shaped by the world we live in. And today's societies are beginning to say that fewer is better and none is just as good.

We haven't just forgotten to have children, we're giving up on the idea altogether.

It's not just Germany that's turning its back on the idea of family. According to Peter McDonald, the one-child family is fast becoming a choice in Russia and some central and eastern European countries. 'You can see that it's a preference because Russians have the first child fairly early by western standards and they don't have any after that so obviously they are controlling for fertility after the first,' he said in an interview. So, too, the Chinese, who had the one-child family forced on them, are now developing a preference for it. Says McDonald, 'The one-child family may have been imposed upon them but over time they get used to it. There's discussion now about lifting the one-child policy but if they did, it wouldn't make much difference to the birth rate because they've got this value inculcated in society over twenty or so years. It becomes part of their value system.'[5]

Australia still clings to the two-child preference but there are indications that the next generation of potential child-bearers may be less enamoured of the idea of a family. In 2002, the HILDA figures showed that young men were less optimistic about their chances of having children. Of men aged eighteen to 24 years, 27 per cent expected to remain childless, compared with 21 per cent of women. Until recently, the vast majority of young people have both wanted to have children and expected to have children. But if one in four young men don't expect to have children, it becomes difficult to unwind those expectations or spark their desire to be dads. Although our expectations of having children change throughout our lives, these expectations are the bedrock of whether we'll have kids and how many we'll have. As Ruth Weston from the Australian Institute of Family Studies says in an interview:

> *Expectations are really important. In the 60s and 70s there was a preference for three and four children; in the 90s this moved down to two or three and now more people are likely to say two and sometimes one. The social norm helps shape the expectations of the next generation.* [6]

The one-child family or no-child family is still not popular in Australia, but as actual sizes of families decrease, expectations are lowered and eventually desires change.

The ways in which societies become intolerant of children have not been explored much, if only because it appears to be such a new phenomenon. On a personal level, it's possible to see it when you take a pram and a toddler through a child-scarce society. Amble through an inner city suburb of DINKs and empty-nesters and see how easy it is to get in and out of shops, to find a bus in off-peak hours and then see how the cafe proprietor greets the family when the place is full of adults reading the paper. Take the kids to those spa towns of Germany that are full of retirees and see how many of the spas are open to children. Go to the parks of Bilbao and see how the playing fields are full of adult soccer players. On a macro level, the disappearance of children will make authorities deaf to the needs of the family. It's harder for a parent to argue for a work-based childcare centre in a company that has few parents on board; it is difficult for parents to push governments to devote funds to families when the majority of their voters are over 50 and agitating for gourmet meals-on-wheels. Even governments desperate for a working population will find it difficult to institute family policies in a country of old couples and young DINKs. And the attitude of society towards children does influence fertility. A negative view of children sets up a peer pressure for those considering it. And a society that's blind to the needs of children creates a landscape that's difficult to steer a pram across.

A synthesis report on the 2000 meeting of the Austrian Institute for Family Studies said, 'A general sense that a society is child-orientated or child-friendly probably has some effect on raising thresholds (of fertility)'. It added, 'If children are always portrayed as a negative (a threat to a good relationship, an obstacle to having a good time, as potential drug addicts or delinquents) or if social institutions don't make allowances for the possibility that a person has children (No Dogs, No Children Allowed) then thresholds will tend to be lower.'[7]

No Dogs, No Children. The sign is seen often enough outside clubs, pubs, casinos and adult sports venues. But how soon will we see it outside cafes, restaurants, workplaces and health resorts? And how soon will we carry those words around in our own minds?

According to the UN, most countries believe their fertility is unacceptably low when it gets under 1.5. At present, there are 26 countries that have indicated to the UN that their rates are too low. Australia—at 1.7—isn't officially worried, mainly because there is widespread acceptance of relatively high levels of immigration. But our population is already shifting into lower growth patterns because of the continual erosion of fertility. This is compounded by the fact that the baby boomers have passed their child-bearing years, there are fewer women in child-rearing years and even fewer just coming into their fertile lives. Moreover, many believe we will inevitably shift to lower levels of fertility on an individual level. Says McDonald, 'There are places that are like Australia—Canada and Scotland, for example—where fertility is going under 1.5 so there's a possibility we might follow them down to those sort of levels.' Even if current trends continue, the women who are now reaching the end of their fertile lives will find that 22 per cent of them are childless, 16 per cent have had only one child, 35 per cent have had two, 20 per cent three and 5 per cent four children.

As demographers point out, a childless rate of even 22 per cent is not so unusual historically—one in five women who were born at the end of the nineteenth century didn't have children—but the downsizing in families is new. The biggest decline has been in big families; there's been a small decrease in families with three children and a substantial rise in one-child families.

To date, the downsizing in families has been treated as an aberration. It has been said that once women get over their post-liberation phase, they'll get back to producing families; that once women learn about the dangers of delaying families, they'll start having babies earlier; that once they get a break in the work–life balance, they'll be happier to enter motherhood. There's an idea that once blokes get over their commitment problems, they'll settle down earlier; that once men don't have to work so hard, they'll show more of an interest in kids; that once unskilled men get more job security, they'll take on the responsibility of family. Certainly, family-friendly policies have had a positive impact on family formation in other countries. As McDonald says:

Put good policy in place and fertility may stay where it is. That's what happened in Europe. In the early 80s, fertility rates in Europe didn't vary too much—1.7 to 1.8—and since that time some countries have instituted highly supportive family policies and others haven't and *there's almost a perfect correlation today with where their fertility rates are—those with good policies stayed at that level, those that didn't have seen them drop to 1.3 and 1.2.*[8]

Australia is still in the early years of low fertility—it has been in the negative zone since the mid-70s but it only backtracked strongly in the 90s. With good policy, we might not enter the downward spiral that has overtaken much of Europe and, indeed, parts of Asia. But there is a possibility that we are moving beyond the aberrant, that our behaviour isn't a deviation from the norm but the start of something new. We may well be building a new sort of society—one that will calcify into a child-unfriendly place.

The new reality is redefining how we make relationships—how we hook-up, break up, move in and move out of intimate relationships. It is changing the period when we settle down to marriage, careers, mortgages and family. It is redefining when we think is a good time to have children and it's changing the concept of family.

Johanna Wyn of Melbourne University's Australian Youth Research Centre believes we have just invented a form of adulthood. 'People tend to look at the lives of these young people and think they are enjoying an extended youth. It's not an extended youth, it's a different way of seeing life. The previous generation aimed to get it right, this generation knows they must be responsive and flexible. The best scenario for them is to have the option to move on and that shapes their lives around uncertainty,' she says in an interview.

Her ongoing survey of youth found that by the age of 30, only 13 per cent of them had had babies, only a third were married and many were surprised at the way their lives were turning out. 'Quite a few are surprised they haven't found a partner and they were quite regretful about that. Most want to have kids and they're shocked that this is the way it's panned out, they thought it would be better by now.' Obviously many of the respondents had cherished the idea of having a family but their lives had taken a turn that surprised not just the older generation, but many of the youth. They did have family but it didn't look like the family that was in their imagination. These youth often have family-like structures in their lives but these are provided by their network of friends and their closer connections with their birth families. This extended relationship with their first families extends beyond the free board. Wyn says:

> *Their family of origin is important to most of them—it's not about starting your own family but keeping your links with your birth family and many are reliant on them for support—not just financial support but emotional support. They have established new forms of friendships with their parents.*

To date, this extended period of youth has split adulthood into two distinct periods—an early, commitment-free, independent and mobile period and a later, more condensed period where all those commitments of partnership, mortgages, children and career are tackled. Wyn isn't sure that this generation of 30-year-olds will take on the second period of adulthood too rapidly. 'For people in their mid-twenties and early thirties, this pattern of being mobile in work, valuing experiences and emphasising lifestyle and well-being, probably won't change until they're in their mid-fifties and, even then they might not change.'

When asked about the implications for family and fertility from this generation, Wyn is blunt: 'We're not going to get many babies out of them, that's for sure.'[9]

Young adulthood is not the only area that has been redefined. We are shifting our concept of the ideal time to have children. As the fertility experts warn, our ideas of when we want children and the ideal time for our bodies to have them are out of sync. Robert Norman of Adelaide University put it succinctly when he said, 'What we're doing is moving the desired fertility age into the biologically inappropriate age'. Whereas the brides of the 50s and 60s had their first child before they turned 25, and the partners of the 70s and 80s began having children in their late twenties, the cultural norm is now to have children in the early thirties. If the ideal time to have children stretches out to the mid- to late thirties, then we're going to need many more fertility clinics.

If our idea of when it's a good time to have babies can shift so radically in such a short period of human history and if our idea of what adulthood means can be redefined within the space of a generation, it doesn't take much imagination to see how our concept of the ideal family can also change—must also change.

Both the size and shape of families are undergoing constant renovation—the sit-com ideal of Mum and Dad with kids at home now represents less than half of all families. One in six families are single-parent units and gay partnerships are almost as common as extended family groupings. But one part of the family ideal has remained relatively constant—the idea of children. This may be about to change.

There is anecdotal evidence that the one-child family is becoming a goal for two-career families. These couples generally have children later—often in the late thirties—so their biological chances of having fewer children are greater and they also have more to lose by being out of the workforce a number a times. Some have unkindly referred to such babies as the accessory baby. One in six women now ends up having just one child, but for most this is still largely a disappointment—because of relationship break-ups, fertility problems or economic hardship. But in an increasingly child-unfriendly society, it may become a popular preference.

The seismic shifts that are currently reshaping families have been called post-modern—if only because it is fluid, uncertain and hard to describe. But it should be called the post-capitalist family because so many of its characteristics have been formed in the wake of rampant capitalism. Post-capitalist youth are those who have responded to the insecure workforce and the consumption-orientated society by keeping their lives free of commitment, their careers changeable and their options open. As Johanna Wyn says, 'Companies have told us all of the need to be flexible, they've got rid of these ideas of permanence and loyalty and the kids have responded in a very practical way—they make sure that they have the capability of moving on.' Youth have reacted to the globalisation of trade, economics and politics by streaming into the global cities of the world for work and education. They are creatures of popular media—friends of *Friends*, Seinfeldesque in attitude and as adaptable as Will and Grace.

The two-career family is also a post-capitalist unit. The working parents' jobs were born in the explosion of jobs through the 80s and 90s and they've buckled under the subsequent intensification of work. Under such work pressure, the two-career couple have scaled down their family size to better suit the expanded demands of their jobs. When the two-career family needs more support, they go to the marketplace to solve the problem. They outsource child caring, cleaning, cooking and tutoring. And because the two-income family spends so much on services, both of them must stay in the 24/7 workforce to pay for it all.

The working-class man has been redefined by those economic changes of the 80s and 90s. He has been turfed out of those permanent, full-time jobs that once paid enough to support a whole family. He now finds himself in insecure, casual employment that barely keeps him clothed, much less feeding a family. With little to offer a partner or children, he is locked out of marriage and family.

And for the majority of people, the post-capitalist family is shaped around the demand of the job and the dictates of the market. One has a full-time job and the other a part-time job and family life fits into the crevices of work and domestic responsibilities. A pregnancy is hidden until the last moment; maternity leave is cobbled together with holidays, savings and long-service leave and another pregnancy (if there is to be one) is rushed into so there won't be too many breaks from the job. Child care is structured around the ever-expanding work shift and then there's a decade of sneaking out to see children at carnivals, taking sick leave to tend children and leaving an old coat over the back of the chair so the boss won't remember that you have another life tucked away in the crevices.

In a post-capitalist world, we don't work to live, we live to work and everything gets referred back to the market. The market ideology becomes the reference point for every decision, the same way that religion was once the touchstone for decisions. Can I afford this yet? Will the patter of little feet, prevent my next step up the ladder? How can I take on a life-long commitment when I don't know what my shifts are next week? If you listen too long to the answers of the marketplace, you baulk at the idea of children and if you don't have children in your life, or on the street, or in your imagination, then you go off the idea altogether.

The lie of the land

When I left school, the first thing I wanted to do was set up a share household, where half a dozen mates could party hard and hang loose outside the confines of suburbia. For my generation this dream took us to inner city hovels with outside toilets, sheets across windows and moneyboxes by the phone. When my children talk of life after school, they get out the atlas. Two years in London would be nice. A year studying in Dublin would be fun. A stint of volunteer work in Sri Lanka would be a blast. In their imagination, the future lies beyond the border of Australia.

The disappearance of children from our homes, our communities and our future is creating ripples across the world. There are already fewer children in schools across the developed world; there will be fewer young workers within the next decade and fewer parents in the next generation. But it's the distribution of young and old that will have the most obvious and immediate impact on the globe. Like environmental management, population is not just a numbers game; it's a management game.

In the developed world, there are already well-established pockets of aging and population decline. Russia, for instance, has been losing population since the collapse of communism in 1990. With a birth rate of 1.3, a declining life expectancy and emigration, Russia loses between 750 000 and one million citizens a year. They are literally written off the demographic pyramid. Even President Vladmir Putin has referred to his country as a 'decaying nation'. In Estonia, where the birth rate is 1.4, the president told his citizens on the New Year of 2003, 'Let us remember that in just a couple of decades the number of Estonians seeing the new year will be one-fifth less than today'. Japan, with a birth rate of 1.3 and virtually no immigration, should start losing population in 2005. Commentators there have dubbed this century as the 'silver century' because there will be one million Japanese centenarians (people aged 100-plus) by the middle of the century. China's success in implementing a one-child family policy hasn't just stalled their population increase and aged the population, it's created a surplus of males. Because of widespread use of sex selection technology there are an estimated 20 million more adult males than females. Some commentators have suggested that the surplus of males will make for a deficit of peace and the Chinese government may be tempted to conscript many of the men into the military to absorb their energies. While there are several examples through history of large populations of surplus women because of war, there's isn't much history of excessive numbers of men. Two societies that did have a temporary excess of men—convict Australia and the Wild West of America—certainly weren't healthy societies.

All these national trends are occurring within a world population that is still growing so the demographic decay is sometimes difficult to appreciate. But population growth has been slowing for more than a decade and in most of the world it's not starving babies in the

Third World that are affecting the statistics but aging retirees. According to UN projections made in 2000, the world population will stabilise at 9 billion within 40 years. It's worthwhile noting that the UN projections just four years earlier put the likely population at 10 billion and six years before that the projection stood at 14 billion. As couples unwind their ambitions for a family, the UN follows shortly after with another lowering in projected populations. By the mid-century the world's birth rate will fall below replacement, populations will reach a plateau and, over the next generation or so, populations will start to shrink. But even before the world reaches its apex of human population, the composition of the population will be radically different from the one we know today.

The explosion in longevity has replaced the population explosion as a cause of worldwide concern. Except in a few places—parts of Africa, India and Russia—people are living longer. Our failure to reproduce ourselves and our cleverness at surviving is creating a century of the old. In Japan the average age will be 53 years within a few decades, in Europe it will be 52, in Australia the late forties and even in a relatively fertile United States it will be 40-something. Countries which have had five or six workers supporting every retiree will experience such as sharp decline in young populations that there will be 2.5 workers supporting each retiree, and in some European countries this ratio will edge down to one worker supporting each retiree.

Unlike the population explosion, which sparked numerous doomsday predictions, the reaction to the aging and moribund population trends has been mostly relaxed and comfortable. This is understandable on a few levels. First, it won't be as dramatic as a population explosion. In 1968, Paul Ehrlich's book, *The Population Bomb*, warned that the world was going to run out of food within a matter of a few years. It never happened. Compared to the challenge of feeding, clothing and housing millions of extra people within the space of a few years, a slow erosion of population—whether on a world level or country level—is easier to manage. It could be argued that the world won't end with a bang but a whimper.

But the relaxed mood may also be a result of the fact that the baby strike has created big economic gains in many countries. As Phillip Longman writes in The Empty Cradle, the lack of dependents in countries like Japan and South Korea and Germany freed up people, resources and capital during the 80s and 90s and helped create economic booms.[1] But these countries were building up a generational debt. In much the same way that governments can build up fiscal debts that eventually become untenable for future generations, these countries have been building up a demographic debt. Their failure to invest in youth for the future will come with compound interest.

Even in Australia with a higher fertility rate than most of Europe and relatively high immigration, the business of keeping the numbers steady—or growing—will prove a huge challenge. As Peter McDonald says in an interview:

> On present levels population will grow—mainly through aging—to 25–26 million and then level off to zero growth and if you're happy with that scenario then migration around the present level and fertility where it is will be acceptable. If you want a rapidly growing population, you will need much greater migration but I think those days of high population growth have passed. Even a growth of 1.2 to 1.5 (roughly today's rate) is near impossible to sustain. You'd have to have a huge migration rate of two-and-a-half times the rate we have now.[2]

Such a rate would require us to build a new city the size of Canberra every eighteen months.

The rate of population growth may affect the sales of houses, cars and tissues but it's the characteristics of the population that will prove more of a headache for government and business. The aging of Australia was highlighted in the *Intergenerational Report* by the Treasury in 2002—a report which attempted to put the looming demographic crunch on the political agenda. Within 40 years, the report said, the ratio of very old (85 years-plus) will jump from 1.5 per cent to 4 per cent; the ratio of retirees (65 years-plus) will double. On present trends, workforce participation will decline from 64 per cent to 55 per cent and those eligible for the pension will increase from 2.7 million to 6.3 million people.[3] The aging of the population will put enormous strains on either government coffers or the working population. Either spending is cut or taxes go up or the aged pay for their own retirement or all of the above happens.

There are ways of lessening the impact of aging. Superannuation contributions could rise so the large population of aged can finance their own retirement; we could encourage the aged to stay in the workforce and get more mothers into the workforce; we could raise productivity levels or we could live with much higher levels of immigration. But immigration doesn't make a big impact on the aging profile because most migrants are the same age as the average Australian—36 years. As the average Australian ages, the average immigrant will be younger and will help lower the average age, but immigration obviously doesn't have nearly the same impact as babies on the aging profile.

The reality of the aging population profiles of the world is that even if most wanted fewer people on the planet, many countries can't afford it. We are going to enter lower growth periods over the next half century and, even though many might be happier with lower standards of living, this low-growth period will come at a high cost. An aging, low-growth population doesn't just mean fewer new cars sold, less building construction and more industries running at idle: it means less vitality in both economies and societies. Old countries don't innovate, they don't take risks, they look inwards and settle for low returns. They conserve capital rather than create businesses. In 2002 the London School of Business and Babson College released an index of entrepreneurial activity across the globe and found that old countries don't rank as highly as young ones. Countries such as India and China, which have about five working-age people to every retired person were the most entrepreneurial countries in the world, whereas countries like Japan and France, which have the lowest ratios of working-age to retired, were among the least entrepreneurial. In an age when human capital is becoming the most important foundation of business, where innovation and creativity drive profits, productivity and growth, this dead hand of aging will lay heavily on capital. Either the aging will have to change their outlook or commerce will have to settle for lower growth rates. Either way, the young and educated will become precious commodities.

Books like Richard Florida's *The Rise of the Creative Class* have explored how cities and regions have been reinvigorated simply by the arrival of young, educated and creative people. Places like Austin and Seattle in the United States, Paris and London and Sydney have attracted global citizens who create eco-systems of innovative businesses.[4] It's no longer the countries with coal seams, ports or cheap manufacturing that rule the world but countries with talent. And unlike coal mines and ports, talent can pack its bags and move across the world and, increasingly, that's what it's doing. The shift of people across the globe is a crucial aspect of population trends. As demographers see it, the world is being divided into winners and losers. The losers fail to attract migrants and they'll see their youth take off for more promising parts of the world; their industries will start shutting down; the towns and countryside will empty; infrastructure won't be maintained; services will be wound back and aging residents will live in virtual ghost towns. The winners, like the cities mentioned above, will attract youth from around the country and the world; they'll become destination cities for migrants and industry; their infrastructure will strain and often services won't keep up with demand, but their young residents will live in economic island paradises. When children like mine open the atlas of the world and pinpoint the places they'd like to go, you can bet that most of those places are the demographic winners—places with youth on their side.

For some countries this demographic decline is not in the future, it's happening now. As I write, the New York Times has published a report on the decay of Dresden in east Germany. Since the collapse of the Berlin wall in 1990, the population of east Germany has dropped from 16.7 million to 15.1 million. A low birth rate and the flight of youth to other parts of the world has turned old communist housing blocks into high-rise ruins. As the New York Times article said, 'Economic stagnation, chronic unemployment and a dwindling population have turned many of the eastern neighbourhoods into ghost towns. Dresden, the majestic, if faded, capital of the state of Saxony, plans to close 43 schools this summer because of a dearth of children.'[5]

Australia already has winners and losers in the demographic stakes and this divide will grow sharper. The population is on the move and, mostly, it's moving away from places that need it most and into the places that need it the least. The winners are Sydney, Melbourne and southeast Queensland. In Queensland, most growth comes from internal migration and, while many of the seachangers are older, there is enough of a mix to ensure reasonable growth for the foreseeable future. Melbourne and Sydney are attracting youth from around Australia and from around the world. In the five years to 2001, 45 per cent of Sydney's population growth came through immigration and in Melbourne 47 per cent. Craig Shepherd at National Economics, compiler of the *State of the Regions* report, has said that Australia is developing a migratory culture similar to that of the United States where households routinely move across the continent in search of economic prosperity. 'Australians historically don't like to move, they have an attachment to place that other countries don't have. But they're moving now. They're developing lifestyle migration patterns that are driven by economic opportunities,' he said in 2003.[6]

The migrations that are cleaving Australia are twofold. First, the major cities are retaining their young populations and soaking up youth from rural, regional and smaller cities. At the other end of the ledger, older residents are staying put in rural towns that are losing their youth, their talent and their services. Some of the older population of both cities and the bush move to lifestyle areas and so are creating pockets of pensioner postcodes along the coast of Australia.[7]

Such is the lure of the big city lights, that it has reversed the nationwide aging trend within city cores. According to City of Sydney figures, Sydney CBD's average age from 1997 to 2001 has dropped from 32 to 31 years. The average age for the whole of Sydney has risen from 33 to 34 years and the national has moved up from 34 to 35 years.

Those losers in the demographic stakes are already agitating for change. In November 2003 a national population summit was held in Adelaide as civic leaders sought answers to the state's demographic losses. Describing the state as the canary down the coal mine, the conference speakers told of how the state's population was aging faster, the proportion of retirees to working age people was blowing out sooner and the population could begin to decline within twenty years. On a projection by the Australian Bureau of Statistics, the most likely population for South Australia by the mid-century is for 50 000 fewer residents—most of whom will disappear from the countryside. Some of the ramifications of this include smaller markets, less viable businesses and fewer jobs; decaying public infrastructure, falling property prices, cuts to services and lower investment. Not too many civic leaders of the wine state believe that low growth is good for the environment. Indeed, South Australia has lobbied the federal government for more migrants and an expansion of assisted migration programs which give incentives to migrants to settle in regional areas.

South Australia is the canary down the coal mine not just for population decline but for demographic war. Like many countries around the world, the state is now looking at ways to boost its population of young workers. So far, the global demographic war for talent has been concentrated on workers—the temporary migrants who live and work in Australia for a year to two, rather than the permanent arrivals. During the 90s, temporary movements of people in and out of Australia became so numerous that they exceeded the movements of the permanent arrivals and departures. In the space of a decade, the impact of the global guest worker was huge. By 2003, there were one million Australians living and working overseas. But the flow into Australia of temporary workers is even greater. In 2003, 184 000 foreigners arrived in Australia intending to stay for a year or so, while 86 000 Australians left our shores for a few years. These relatively young workers filled jobs in hospitality, law, property, IT, teaching and nursing and filled suburbs like Bondi and Brunswick with international accents. One of the demographers to track globalisation's ghost migrants, the University of Adelaide's Graeme Hugo, said in an interview that the shift represented 'a huge change in immigration policy, from permanent to temporary migration'. But Australia isn't the only country swapping its young population with the world. As Hugo said, 'Whereas in the past only the United States, Canada and Australia had substantial migration programs, now every European country has a skilled migration program. England now has a bigger migration program than Australia.'[8]

As countries continue to age, they will increasingly want to grab bigger shares of the youth worker market. Countries have already expanded their working holiday arrangements and are likely to shape their permanent migration programs more and more around young, skilled people. For Australia's spread of population, this will further concentrate populations in the two global cities. Sydney and Melbourne not only attract the majority of permanent migrants but the majority of temporary migrants. They also attract most of the young from around Australia and when those young people decide to have families, they'll have them in the capital cities. A decade or so ago, natural population increase was spread quite widely across the country—the youth of Wagga Wagga had families in town, Adelaide youth had their kids there and so on. But as more youth move to the cities, so too do their future families. Also, once in the city, they may well have fewer kids, as the city birth rate of 1.6 lags behind that of the rural areas, where it's still at replacement level. So the micro demographic changes are making the macro changes more intense. More youth move to cities, they have their families there but they have fewer children than they would have had if they'd stayed in their birthplace.

As globalisation continues and world borders become more permeable—at least to the young and talented—the gyrations of populations will become even more pronounced. Global cities, especially those that are attractive to the creative class, will be the winners and old economy cities the losers. But above and beyond this are two giant players in the people-moving game, India and China. Both are becoming economic powerhouses and both are producing bigger pools of skilled workers. China's ability to supply the world with workers will be hampered by its aging profile—it may be happy to take jobs from the world but less happy about supplying workers to the world. India, however, with a fertility rate of three is in a better position. Its population is still growing and much of this growth is coming from the bottom—babies—rather than the top—more aged. With an English-speaking culture and a commitment to higher education, India is making the one product that will be in short supply globally—a well-educated, English-speaking, young workforce. In the next 40 years India alone will produce another 400 million workers and that, as Peter McDonald points out, is enough to satisfy the shortage of workers that will be experienced across the world.

India will be the nursery of the world. It will provide the world with workers for much of the 21st century. The only question is whether India will provide these workers on their own homeland or send them off into the lands of the aged. Will 400 million Indians fan out across the world in what would be the biggest migration in history or will the jobs go to the young and productive continent of India?

The practice of going offshore, or 'offshoring' as management consultants refer to it, is growing rapidly. Asian economic zones have long handled the cheap manufacturing for the world but at the end of the 90s more sophisticated jobs began going to India and China. Professional services, such as IT management and programming, data input, call centres and book-keeping shifted offshore and they were followed by jobs at higher levels in medical analysis, financial advice, editing, architectural services and even some public services. In 2003, the US firm A.T. Kearney predicted that 8 per cent of the jobs in the American finance industry would shift offshore within five years. Virtually any job that is computer-based or phone-based can be done remotely—whether that's down the road or across the other side of the world.

For those who think of the starving people in India when the subject of population arises, it will be a surprise when India's greatest legacy—a population of young, educated workers—comes to the rescue of a demographically impoverished world. That doesn't alter the fact that India still has problems feeding all its people—20 per cent are undernourished—but the much bigger story is how India has created a population of middle-class, educated youth in a greying world.

One way or another, parents always lose their children. In the past they lost them to marriage, the cloisters, the military, apprenticeships and even to slavery. This generation of parents is more likely to lose their children to migration than to anything else. Whether it's the 18-year-old Mount Isa girl who goes to Brisbane for university, or the Melbourne lawyer who shifts to London for a two-year stint or the east German engineer who moves to Dublin for a five-year contract, the world's youth is on the move.

Knitting bootees for the country

After a friend had a baby, I went to the newsagency to buy a card. I made my way past the enigmatic Gary Larson, witty 30th birthday cards, cruelly funny 50th cards and found myself in a floral corner. For Mother. It was a veritable library of lavender landscapes, bouquets of blue irises, pink ribbons, goofy kids, garden scenes and sunsets smudged with sentimental prose. Why aren't there any cards for mothers like those witty 30th birthday cards? Greeting cards are something of an SMS message to those we love and the categories of cards in the newsagency reflect the sort of relationships that are common in society today. I noted, for instance, there are now categories for multiple births, step-parents and 100-year-olds. But motherhood is still stuck in the image of blue irises and purple prose. I thought of all those images of mother I'd come across in writing this book. Those pictures of blue irises were redolent of Offred's prison in *The Handmaid's Tale*. The pictures of pink ribbons reeked of Betty Friedan's 50s housewife. The goofy kids could have stepped off the set of *Malcolm in the Middle* and onto a Hallmark card.

Then I remembered what Adrienne Rich wrote about the ancient worship of women in her book, *Of Woman Born*. The figurine of a pregnant woman etched in stone was the symbol of bounty, power and spirituality and, said Rich, it may have represented the high point in history for mothers. A card featuring a fat, pregnant chick from the Bronze Age would have done the trick nicely. I settled for a field of lavender.

Motherhood is no longer a given. A motherhood issue may still mean something that everyone agrees is *worthy*, but motherhood itself is no longer something that everyone agrees is *worthwhile*. Motherhood has lost status and meaning; it has been curtailed and made Lite; it has been delayed, parodied and pitied; it keeps getting locked behind a picket fence even while it's being written out of the future. It may be preserved on a Hallmark card but it's endangered everywhere else.

Community leaders—mostly in government and business—have been happy to ignore family as long as it didn't affect their core operation. There has been an assumption that what goes on behind the bedroom door doesn't belong in policy; that people will make their own decisions about having children without any interference from government or business. But that was when those bedroom decisions were still producing roughly two children per couple and immigration could be relied upon to pick up the slack. Behind that hands-off approach was the assumption that women would have babies no matter what; that is was hard-wired into people to reproduce themselves; that apart from disturbances like war and depression, populations would continue to increase; that fertility might not be God-given, but it was a given. They forgot that women now have choice.

The fact that populations are aging and will soon decline has forced governments and business to put demography on their agenda. Around the world national governments and some companies are taking action, if only to ensure they have enough taxpayers and workers for the next generation. Many of these initiatives are being examined in Australia as governments try to prevent the country falling into the demographic black hole that has opened up in the developed world. As of mid-2004, schools were beginning to tussle with the prospect of fewer primary school children walking through their gates. As this decade unfolds secondary private schools will have to grapple with the issue of fewer teenagers; then universities will face sparse student populations; then employers will find fewer Australians lining up for jobs. The economic headcount is under way but what might be more of a challenge is changing the social attitudes about having and raising children. The images of carefree singles and careless parents haunt decisions about having children. The young and childless are forced to choose between a *Friends* lifestyle and joining the Simpsons on the couch. Those nomads of globalisation are more at home in an email address than in suburbia. Those mobile workers can manage flexibility, independence and self-motivation but they can't manage to get a pram around that schedule. As the world opens up to new generations, the prospect of family narrows. The young have been born into smaller families, raised on singles TV shows and inculcated with the idea that they must keep their options open. They'll determine the shape of the next generation and their choices will impact not just their own lives but the lives of their parents' generation and the shape of future generations. It is their decision that may turn pyramid population graphs into coffin shapes.

In the past, Australian governments supported people's decision to have children through tax deductions and child endowments, but more especially through the concept of the family wage. The industrial system set wages, not on the ability of employers to pay, but according to what was required to support a wife and children and the level of skill needed for the job. This began to shift in the early 80s when wages began to be determined by market forces, not family needs. Although the Labor governments of the 80s established childcare centres and helped women into the workforce, help for raising children diminished. The Coalition governments since the late 90s withdrew support further. There were modest initiatives, mainly aimed at keeping women with young children at home but the cost of raising children was privatised further. By the turn of the 21st century, inner-city parents with two children were facing weekly childcare bills of $700; working hours were blowing out and many parents faced 24 years of supporting children through school and university and then into the insecure work environment.

By 2004, Treasury officials had begun whispering into the ear of the federal government that demographic changes meant they should encourage women into the workforce, not reward them for staying at home. Support for raising children is now aimed at enabling women to combine work and care but, compared with efforts in other countries, that help has been superficial and largely aimed at convincing mothers to get a little job. Both major political parties in Australia have programs to provide new mothers with a baby bonus and give families some tax benefits. When the Coalition government expanded its baby bonus scheme in 2004, the reaction was mostly positive but there was a feeling that this should be just the first step in a much wider range of supports. There was also criticism that the scheme was focused on keeping women in pocket money jobs, as it was mostly aimed at households where one parent earned 80 per cent of the income and the other 20 per cent. Perhaps the most significant part of the bonus was that it signified that governments have a role in supporting all women who have a child—whether they pursue traditional roles or more modern ones. By the time the federal election was being fought in October 2004, both major political parties were competing to offer families support for raising children. But much of this was done in the spirit of one-up-manship rather than with an eye to a sustainable future. The parties had heard the cries from suburban Australia but the framing of the policy promises were shaped around impressing swinging voters. Offers on child care and family rebates fell well short of international standards and also failed to address the key need of more flexibility in the workplace for parents. For instance, no Australian political party has committed to what is internationally considered a fundamental support for parents—universal paid maternity leave. As of 2002, 62 per cent of Australian women workers didn't have access to paid maternity leave and most of those were in the less privileged parts of the workforce. The average period of paid maternity leave was eight weeks, which is short of the international standard of fourteen weeks. The Human Rights and Equal Opportunity Commission report of 2002, 'Valuing Parenthood', pointed out that nineteen of Australia's top twenty trading partners provide maternity leave and of the 30 countries that make up the OECD, only Australia and the United States fail to provide paid maternity leave.[1]

The search for role models around the world has been a frustrating exercise. The early successes in Scandinavian countries have not proved sustainable (birth rates hover around 1.6 now). France is one of the few countries that has managed to *raise* its fertility level from 1.7 to a healthier level of 1.9 through a comprehensive program of supporting children. But market-dominated countries may find the French way too expensive. In brief, France has 30 different allowances for family, ranging from straight allowances to housing supports; the rights of the family to care for relatives has been written in labour law, tax and social security laws; paid maternity leave is between sixteen and 26 weeks; there are pension benefits to reward parents for their care work; there's free child care and tax deductions that allow parents to claim back 50 per cent of the cost of nannies. What's interesting about the French way is that these supports have been in place for decades; they are across all spectrums of society and they reflect a fundamental belief in the social good of children. In a piece for the *Journal of Population and Social Security*, the academic Marie-Thérèse Letablier, wrote: 'Children are seen as part of the nation; they are a "common good" and the wealth of the nation, which, in return, has obligations towards them.'[2]

This presumption that children are important for national health and wealth took Hillary Clinton by surprise when she visited France in 1989 and 'saw what happens when a country makes caring for children a top priority'. In her book, *It Takes a Village*, Clinton wrote of the exchanges she had with French leaders.

> 'How,' I asked, 'can you transcend your political differences and come to an agreement on the issue of government-subsidised child care?' One after another of them looked at me in astonishment. 'How can you not invest in children and expect to have a healthy country?' was the reply I heard over and over again.[3]

Another interesting aspect of the French system is that it has been changed a number of times to reflect both national and personal priorities. After the war, it was aimed at boosting the population for military purposes; during the early 80s, it was redesigned as a system for helping women into the workforce and more recently it has been changed to accommodate the work–life balance. While Australians were stopping barbecues with talk about the work–life balance, the French reduced full-time work hours to 35 hours a week—a move which has resulted in both mothers and fathers saying they spend more time with children. As Letablier wrote: 'Consideration of the work–life balance by different policy sectors represents an attempt to alter current values in order to construct a more "children-friendly" and less work-orientated environment for both men and women.' The results in France go beyond the sustainable fertility rate. They are expanding the workforce and enhancing family life for both men and women. Eighty-one per cent of women with one child are in the workforce and 70 per cent of those with two children work. Moreover, the shortening of working hours has meant that the difference in hours between full-time and part-time work has narrowed so paid work is being spread more evenly between men and women. However, even the French programs have had limited impact on how much housework men do—men spend half as much time as women on housework and one-third as much on child care.

In the past decade or so, Australia's social policies have tended to mirror the American way rather than the European way. As Australian governments investigate ways of assisting in the raising of the next generation, they can choose between these two models, which basically reflect public and private schemes.

The recent history of getting institutional support for raising children has largely been one of bickering between government and business about who should pay. Government claims that it can't afford too much 'middle-class welfare' and business claims family support is a government responsibility. Australian political parties are now recognising that they can't afford to ignore their responsibility but business still argues that it is not theirs. Yet business has much to lose from demographic decline, it is partly responsible for the decline and it is increasingly being recognised that it should contribute to the creation of its own human capital. Even Hillary Clinton, the former first lady of that premier capitalist country, concluded her book saying,

I have talked about the responsibilities of individuals and institutions for the future of our children and the village they will inherit. No segment of society has a more significant influence on the nature of that legacy than business . . . our circumstances therefore require new and thoughtful responses from every segment of society, particularly from business.[4]

Business isn't blind to the challenge. At the start of 2004, the *Australian Financial Review* conducted a survey of 29 chief executives on what were the top three challenges facing Australia. In the past these sorts of surveys have produced a fairly predictable list of challenges: productivity, inflation, interest rates, the unions, political stability and currency changes. But the 2004 survey produced a few surprises. More than a third of the CEOs nominated demographic changes as a key concern for business.[5] Demography is destiny for business too.

One of the ways business can contribute to the creation of their future stocks of human capital is through paid maternity and paternity leave. Business already funds paid maternity leave, but it is largely women employed by big companies that receive it. Women in the public service also are entitled to paid maternity leave. As 'Valuing Parenthood' points out, a universal scheme for Australia could be achieved through a number of ways. It could remain employer-funded; it could be achieved through government funding only; it could be done through a social insurance scheme that government and employers contribute to; it could be done through a type of superannuation scheme that government, employers and employees contribute to. The idea of a superannuation scheme for parents would be easier to achieve today because of the widespread acceptance of retirement superannuation schemes. It would also give parents more flexibility for taking leave—sharing it between them, boosting coverage to cater for their lifestyles, taking it over a shorter or longer period and using it to support them through the years of raising a few kids.

While governments and business argue about who should pay for maternity leave, another crucial question is who should get it. Already European countries are extending the concept of maternity leave to paternity leave and a few have extended it further to incorporate general caring leave. Extending leave to both parents and allowing a combination of paid and unpaid leave will get many parents over that most expensive and gut-wrenching childcare period. Many parents are uncomfortable about leaving babies in extended child care and academic opinion also seems to be swinging against the concept.

A further expansion of the policy to cover carers generally recognises the importance of caring, not just for children but for the whole family. Mothers, sons, singles and divorcees will all have caring responsibilities at some stage of their life and these responsibilities will increase further as the population ages and families shrink in size. A childless couple may not have the responsibility of caring for children but, as families downsize, a couple may have total responsibility for caring for four aged parents. Caring at both ends of life—preschool and geriatric—has been outsourced, but some of these roles will come back to the family when there aren't enough paid carers in the community to look after the very old. There will also be less government money to support old age as the population of geriatrics explodes and the population of taxpayers contracts. One way or another, more of the costs and responsibilities of caring will be borne by parents.

The ability of both men and women to be active parents in the early years of their children's lives will take an enormous cultural shift in the workplace. As Barbara Pocock has pointed out, much of the workplace is still designed around the presumption that there is a wife at home; it's still rooted in the idea that the person getting the paycheck is a male breadwinner. The most common family, however, is a dual-income family and workplaces must be renovated to reflect the new reality.

One of the key problems for parents is that the most demanding years at work are also the most demanding years with children. In their early thirties parents find that both bosses and babies want maximum attention. Some writers, in particular Anne Roiphe in the United States, have suggested we should embrace the idea of a fertility oasis around the age of 30. During this period, parents could manipulate hours and periods of work while the children are young without prejudicing their careers. The loss of productivity could be made up by prolonging working lives. Companies are unlikely to accommodate this voluntarily because most have attitudes that favour 30-something-year-olds and discriminate against those over 50. However, government tax policy could encourage companies into less ageist and, indeed, less sexist employment practices. The author of *The Empty Cradle*, Phillip Longman, proposed giving tax relief to parents. He said this could be done through the payroll tax system— where parents with one child had their payroll taxes cut by a third and those with three had the tax eliminated altogether.[6] A similar policy of tax cuts could be applied in Australia. Already Victoria and the ACT exempt payroll tax from maternity leave payments; this could be adopted by all states. But it could also be extended to compensate either parents or companies. A payroll tax deduction could be used to raise the take-home pay of parents, to compensate them for increased child expenses and keep them in the workforce, or it could be directed into company coffers to either encourage the employment of parents or to subsidise family-friendly practices. In this developing era of the triple-bottom line, there are many instruments that governments could use to ensure that companies fulfil not just shareholder desires but those of the broader society (and those of future shareholders).

Lobbyists for business argue that the marketplace economy will solve a lot of these work–life issues because the looming shortage of labour will force companies to compete for workers with better conditions. To a limited extent, this is happening at the top end of town, mostly for prized employees. Those law firms, who have encouraged a late-working culture through free meals, massage and concierge services are now beginning to offer part-time work options for lawyers. The most family-friendly workplaces offer carers' leave, flexible start and finish times, the ability to work from home at least one day a week, part-time options in senior jobs and, most importantly, role modelling from senior people who take up these options. But there are still very few companies that embrace family-friendly policies and even those that often don't have the practices to back them up. Michael Bittman, who examined work cultures both in Australia and the UK in 2003–04 found that even those with good 'cover stories' of flexible work practices didn't walk the talk. The men in those companies saw part-time work as career death and the managers agreed, according to an interview with Bittman in the *Age* newspaper. One manager, asked his reaction to a request for part-time work, said, 'From where I'm sitting now, the red pen would be out'.7

Flexibility in the workplace is a key—perhaps the key—concern for parents. Maternity leave may help a woman settle a baby into the new life and childcare services help get a child through to school, but flexible work makes the lifetime role of parenting easier. Flexibility at work allows parents to care for sick children, to attend sporting carnivals and recitals. It allows parents to model work around the needs of a baby and then change it again to suit a preschooler and then redesign it around the school year.

For the past few decades, companies have created a flexible workforce through the creation of casual and part-time workers. But the flexibility has all been in favour of the company; it's been designed to cater for the flow of business. Flexibility for parents means shaping work around the needs of their children. There are many ways to achieve flexible working conditions for parents and most involve a closer relationship between work and children. This means that children must be brought back into society, in particular the workplace. For some parents, flexibility means being able to work from home. Already one million Australians work at least partly from home. Some companies allow people to work from home one day a week; others allow parents to work from home during holidays or for one or two afternoons a week. The boom in home businesses has been partly driven by this desire for a workable combination of economic and home life. According to Australian Bureau of Statistics figures, there was a 20 per cent increase in the number of women running home businesses in the five years to 2003. There are now 250 000 women conducting businesses at home, mostly in childcare services, property businesses and clerical services. In many ways, these businesses are like the enterprises of pre-industrial times when family units at home did most of the work. Mechanisation took people out of the home into factories but technology is allowing them to return to cottage industry. Even at the top end of town, mobile technology has allowed senior people to work remotely. This has usually meant that executives work from cars, the street, airports and cafes but some are taking advantage of their freedom of movement and work from home one day a week. There are, of course, drawbacks to working from home. I've been a full-time telecommuter since my first daughter was born twenty years ago (my first computer modem was an acoustic coupler that sheathed the phone piece like a giant condom). Working from home has enabled me to stay in close contact with my children while maintaining a writing career. It has, however, meant some jobs weren't open to me, my career was put on a wobbly track, the office social life was remote and my desk manners became feral.

For other working parents, school holidays are the worst period for juggling kids and smuggling time but there are possible solutions to the holiday blues. The public service and some companies have shortened the working year to allow parents to be paid for 48 weeks over 52 weeks, thereby enabling them to take eight weeks' leave. This means parents can take off school holidays. Some companies provide emergency care, which enables parents to work while children are sick or carers are sick. On an informal basis, some companies allow children to come into the workplace, either after school or during holidays.

Such huge cultural shifts in the workplace won't come easily or cheaply and won't come without a change in attitudes. The people at the top mustn't just sign off on family-friendly policies, they must ensure that line managers embrace such policies and they should act as role models for the new way of working. The shifts will also entail a change in attitude among men. The problem of getting fathers to take time off after the birth of a child (instead of increasing their hours) is a worldwide one. Graeme Russell, of Macquarie University who has studied fathers at work for decades, believes that there is more to meeting the challenge of getting fathers more involved in parenting than employers providing family-friendly conditions.[8] Whether men take advantage of such policies (as discussed in Chapter 4) depends as much on their own attitudes to parenting, the willingness of partners to share parenting and whether senior managers provide a role model or not. Role modelling by political leaders and business leaders will help break down the idea that real men work full-time and never take a break. Interestingly, as Europe pushes family-friendly policies, much headline space has been occupied by which political leaders take time off around the birth of babies (Finland probably wins on that score).

Another push will come from the variety of other workers who are interested in more flexible work lives. Westpac has said that it will soon have as many part-time workers on its HR list as full-timers. The part-time workers will not only be parents but those twenty-somethings who are uncommitted to the career track and older workers who are trading down hours as they shift out of the workforce. A change to more flexible career structures would allow single people to schedule study, travel and caring commitments into their lives. This would also alleviate some of the antagonism that develops when working parents are seen to be getting a break at the expense of childless workers.

In the same way that overwork became the mantra for the workplace of the 90s, flexibility may well become the catchword of the future. It remains to be seen on whose terms flexibility is given.

Flexibility doesn't just have to revolve around home and work. All institutions in society can take a bigger role in raising children. Childcare centres could be open more hours of the day and night, not necessarily to offer extended hours but to cater for different working shifts. Parents who work part-time shifts, or get work on short notice, or work into the night at times, or sometimes have to work on the weekend need centres that can cater to these demands. In the past twenty years, work has moved beyond the nine to five period into all hours and days of the week, but most childcare centres still operate on the presumption that care isn't needed beyond eight to six. Schools could help bridge the gaps in caring. Many schools now offer before- and after-school care but these services could be further extended. One inner city girls' school offers boarding not just for regular boarders but for students who might need short-term or occasional boarding if parents are away, sick or over-committed. Libraries, too, are becoming de facto after-school venues for older primary students and secondary students, but their role as informal educators and carers could be enhanced. Many libraries could incorporate a cafe, a play room or an outdoor playground without endangering the quiet of other areas. For older primary school children who no longer want to go to after-school care, libraries could be places they go to do homework, have afternoon tea, read and play. For older students, libraries could become places to study, meet and share a coffee. To encourage reading, libraries could have regular afternoon sessions or shows with authors, performers and teachers. Making space for children in the public domain can be achieved in many institutions. Truly child-friendly workplaces would welcome visits from children. Employers could have entertainment rooms for them, cafes where they can feel welcome and computers they could use for homework. In the IT boom of the late 90s many edgy workplaces introduced entertainment areas, lounges, play equipment and policies that welcomed the family dog into the office. If dogs can come into some workplaces, why not children?

If society's concept of family remains rooted in the nuclear ideal of Mum, Dad and a few kids, we're not going to cope well with the new sort of family that youth are developing. Already that baby-boom version of the family—two parents, four kids—is an oddity. At any one time, only 1 per cent of families in Australia looks like that. Even the single-child family outnumbers the two-child family when snapshots of suburbia are taken. Yet, somewhere in the back of the minds of many people is still an idea that the nuclear family is normal and everything else is a deviation. Under the radar, Australians have been renovating the family but much of this renovation has escaped scrutiny and therefore it hasn't impacted much on public percep-tions. The most obvious ways that the family has been remade is in the rise of the single-parent household and blended households. Even these two expressions disguise the many different ways the people live within these households. And there are many more creative ways of living as family. Here are a few family units that I know of. Two women—best friends but not lovers—are raising a daughter after the death of the husband of one of the women. Two lesbians are raising two children after the marriage of one of them was dissolved. Two gay men are sharing the house with a single mother and they all share in the care of her daughter. A childless woman shares her house with a nephew while he attends university in Sydney. A mother of two regularly takes in a niece, who is having troubles with her family. Parents of four grown children have shared their home with the son's girlfriend for a year. Grandparents are raising their 14-year-old granddaughter, who has had trouble in her own home. Parents of three children share their space with a niece on weekends when she comes out of boarding school.

The reality for a lot of families is that they don't look like the family they see in margarine commercials. Those so-called traditional families often find themselves with non-biological children living with them and many childless people are helping to raise children. In many ways, as historian Michael Gilding has pointed out, we are returning to the sort of families that used to be common in society before World War II. These were families with cousins, grandparents, lodgers, great aunts and servants—they were dynamic places of care, common responsibilities and love. The title of Hillary Clinton's book, *It Takes a Village*, gives another clue to how we once raised children. In the smaller townships of European countries, such as the United States, Australia and Europe, children were allowed to roam in the community from the age of seven years, or even earlier. Implicit in this was the idea that the children belonged to the community and the community belonged to them.

In even smaller and more distant communities—the tribes of early humanity—a child was with its mother until it was weaned, and it was allowed in the greater community of the tribe from toddlerhood. The child was the responsibility of the neighbours, aunts, uncles or whoever was nearby. Closer to home, Aboriginal Australians have a long tradition of close clan groups. Even in remote settlements today, children are not confined to the parental home but move between houses and community activities. Kinship networks are written into the lore of traditional Aboriginal beliefs and are part of the reality of modern Aboriginal communities. It's only recently that we have confined children to the nuclear family. A shift away from the self-contained and often isolated nuclear family will be even more pronounced if today's youth bring their fluid ideas of family into the later stages of adulthood.

Johanna Wyn believes that the networks of friendships and family that youth have developed won't be dumped on the threshold of the chapel. This generation of twenty-somethings has diverse networks of friends and family and while the fluid nature of their relationships has prevented many from thinking of children, they might end up having children within these new networks. Again, popular culture gives a clue about some new ways of raising children. When Rachel and Ross in *Friends* had a baby, they maintained their friendship and their place in the *Friends* group; when Miranda in *Sex and the City* had a child, she remained in the group of girlfriends while trying to sort out her relationship with the baby's father. *Two and a Half Men* tracks how a single father and his laddish brother raise a boy.

But perhaps the most powerful depiction of a modern family was in the book and movie *About a Boy*. This charts the journey of a 12-year-old boy who realises that his family is too thin when his mother continually attempts suicide. He sets out to find a partner for his mum and a father figure for himself and latches onto the most unlikely of choices—a self-indulgent, emotionally castrated bachelor. But by the end of the movie the bachelor has adopted the boy into his life, mum has found a boyfriend, the bachelor has found another single mum to love and the whole unlikely lot settle into Christmas lunch. About a Boy was about a family, but it took family out of the house. It wasn't about who lived in the home but who cared about the boy.

Bringing the wider community into the task and joy of raising children is being done through other measures, such as the mentoring programs which are organised by both community, government and business groups. The idea that both single people and family people should mentor young people, or act as 'uncles' and 'aunts' widens both the concept of family and the concept of singleness. Part of the stigma about being single was the idea that singles aren't caring for others. Many, of course, do care for relatives and many would like the opportunity to share in the raising of children. If single people have been removed from family life, perhaps that's partly because families haven't let them in.

I suspect that if political voices keep trying to push family behind the picket fence, they will simply alienate more people from the idea of having children and forming their own versions of family. Many are reinventing the family, they just need to be recognised for it.

Perhaps, more than anything, we need a new way of thinking about and talking about the most intimate relationships of our lives. We need to develop a language that takes us beyond calculations, rationalisations and the economics of children.

New expressions for the value of children will reassure young people that children have a right to be here; that children aren't a blot on the landscape but the reason for preserving the environment.

A new way of imagining how children will fit into our lives wouldn't have us fearing that we'll be 'wasting the best years of our life' but looking for ways of bringing children into those best years.

A new way of appreciating our biology will mean there won't be so many blokes who sit in front of Professor Robert Norman and say they'll have two eggs put back in because it's quicker and cheaper.

A new language between women won't mask our lives as mothers or perpetrate the myths of motherhood but touch upon the experience of being a mother. When friends ask us what it's really like, we need permission to speak beyond the extra bills, lost sleep and endless juggling and take them into the world of unconditional love and new-found courage and the sheer joy of sharing a young life all over again.

A different approach to mothering will have us walking into a childcare centre and not just asking about hours and the variety of play equipment but asking whether someone will pat our toddler's back if she can't settle down into her afternoon nap.

A new honesty for parents in the workforce acknowledges that sometimes family life will disrupt business; that early meetings are never a good time; and that a child who comes into the office for a visit isn't an insurance liability but a gift of humanity to the organisation.

A public discussion of children in society will bring children out of the cupboard and onto the national agenda so we won't track after the Germans who have become so aloof from children that they no longer want them.

A philosophy of children won't exclude those who don't have children. It can celebrate children without diminishing the lives of those without them and such a philosophy will, at least, result in fewer people turning around at the age of 40 and declaring they forgot to have children.

Don Watson's book, Death Sentence, explored how the language of management and economics has infiltrated the way we speak about all parts of our lives. We seek 'closure' in relationships, we 'write off' friends who are too 'high maintenance' and ask them 'what's the bottom line' when they want a favour.[9] The title of his book implied that managerial speak was the death sentence for language, but it's also a death sentence for the language of love.

Rationality dictates that we choose to stay with someone for as long as that relationship suits us; that we choose to see our brothers and sisters as long as we have something in common with them; that we choose to see our parents when it's mutually convenient and if we fall out with them, we vow to be polite to them on Christmas Day. Under the rational theory model, we choose friends who share our interests and our lifestyles and if we tire of them, we get a new set of friends. But where do children fit into this rational choice model? We know they are a choice that will last, one way or another, for the rest of our lives. We can't change our mind about having them, there's no refund policy, no guarantees. We don't know who they are, we don't know what they'll be like, we don't know whether we'll like them. We don't know who our children are, so how can we choose them? When I was pregnant with my first child, I remember thinking suddenly that if this child inherited all my ugly parts and all the ugly parts of my partner, it would be a pretty ugly sight. And then I thought about all the traits it might inherit from the ancestors and it dawned on me that it could be a very troubled bub. For the first time in my pregnancy, I realised what a leap into the unknown I'd taken.

Most of us will, at some stage, want to have children but when we sit down to think about it, or talk about it with our partner, what reasons do we find for having them? Chances are we'll come up with eleven good reasons not to have children and only three good reasons to have children, like the childless women that philosopher Leslie Cannold interviewed.

You'd think that we'd know by now why we have children. We have, after all, been having them for a long time and for centuries poets, novelists, philosophers and wise old women have written about the love of children. Have we forgotten why we have children?

When she started her PhD research on how women decide whether or not to have children, Cannold presumed there would be rooms full of literature about why we have children. However when she looked, she found nothing, not even in the shelves of philosophy. A pop-academic approach to this question could be to ask Google to find 101 Reasons for Having Kids. The results come up with a Christian woman who has found 101 reasons—but then Google takes you to 101 Reasons to Ride a Harley motorbike. A quick segue in the world of googling sums up the world of choice we face when deciding to have children. The author of *Maternal Desire*, Daphne de Marneffe, pointed out that not only do women have the choice to have children or not but they now have the choice of whether to mother or not. The education, work opportunities and the lifestyle choices that are now open to women, she says, 'have finally created the potential for mothering to be a chosen activity in ways unimaginable for the vast majority of women throughout history and still in many parts of the world today'. But clearly this choice of spending time with our children and allowing ourselves to develop as nurturers is one that many women are uncomfortable about. Says de Marneffe, 'In the current milieu, women rarely perceive their desire to care for their children as intellectually respectable and that makes it less emotionally intelligible as well. On a broader social level, mothers' needs and desire to work and its importance to their self-sufficiency and self-expression get a strong public hearing but mothers' needs and desires with respect to nurturing their children receive comparatively little serious discussion.'[10]

Cannold also believes that the issue of choice has exposed the fact that we don't have a common belief about the worth of children and how they should fit into our lives.

> It's only recently that we've had to justify it. Before there wasn't a choice about having children, people had sex and children followed. It was considered instinctive, a capitulation to baser instincts, it just happened. So we haven't been talking about this for years.

In the past we may have had explanations for the role of children in life, but we didn't have to have reasons for choosing them. Children were either God's way, nature's call, duty to lineage, fulfilment of women or part of a populate-or-perish policy. Those explanations no longer hold true, but we've yet to articulate new reasons for taking the leap into parenthood. Part of this coyness is due to the rational choice model of modern life and part may be a desire not to offend those who don't have children. Cannold is especially concerned about the impact on the childless.

> Part of what holds us back from that conversation is the tension with the childless-by-choice lobby. Often those conversations about the meaning of parenthood degenerates into that negative stigmatisation of people who choose not to have children. It is difficult to say that having children is a moral thing to do without implying that those who choose not to are morally inappropriate. It is possible to say that but it's a difficult concept to hold onto and there's a lot of sensitivity about it. It's only recently that we've stopped castigating people for not having children, we don't want to return to that.

We have been cut adrift from historical explanations for children and are culturally hamstrung talking about a modern philosophy; but perhaps our greatest challenge in bringing children back into our lives is recreating a public language of love. Says Cannold,

> *It's very hard to find words why children are meaningful and yet it's easy to find words for how difficult raising them can be, how tired you are, how little sex you get, there's a common lingo for talking about the problems. But the pleasures of having children are known only to those who have them, so we don't have a common language that everyone shares. The childless can feel very excluded by this.*

As Cannold was completing a book on childless women when we spoke, she attempted to find the words.

> *We shouldn't think that it's morally deficient or irrational to take this leap of faith to commit oneself to the unknown; to say I'm going to do this even if it doesn't turn out as pleasurable or as fulfilling as I might like it to be; to say I'm willing to accept that the meaningfulness of loving is not necessarily contingent on everything going my way. Part of the pleasure of loving and having relationships is that they have unexpected elements.*

Another reason she suggests is that children take us away from the world of materialism, individualism, consumption and rationality and into a world that revolves around deeper values. 'Part of what makes it meaningful is that is a counter to the world we know, it's a haven in a world that is narrow and materialistic. It takes us out of those values and at some deep level we know that there's a reason to feel proud of ourselves when we take that leap and we know we are doing something good when we stick with it.'

Cannold admits she had difficulty in finding these words.

It took me two hours today to write the paragraph that I just described to you—about this notion of trust and taking a leap of faith. It was there for me but it was buried, so in some ways it's just a question of people like me taking the time to think this out and put it into words. We do need words to conceptualise what we may know in our hearts but are not things we necessarily trust in our heads, which is where we think we should be operating from.[11]

Like Leslie Cannold, I have struggled throughout this book to find words for something that has been the most meaningful part of my life. It has been a struggle between trying not to sound smug and trying not to do a poor imitation of a Hallmark card (if that's possible). It's hard to say your children have helped you become a better person without sounding as if you're pretty pleased with yourself. It's hard to talk of raising children who turn out to be fabulous people without sounding as if you're applying for a medal. It's almost impossible to relate those joyful moments of being with children without sending single friends off to the bar for another drink. Even sharing those Kodak moments with other parents risks spoiling the evening. Parents learn to bite their tongues when they see a child first walk, crack a joke or swim underwater and feel that rush of discovery and delight all over again. They stay mum when they see a picture of a great-grandfather that looks exactly like their boy and they realise how the child is woven into a long ancestry, that the young child is part of a puzzle of history, genetics, chance and tradition. I have bitten my tongue when talking with childless people about family and I realise that they are speaking in the past tense and I'm speaking in the future tense—for me, family is in the future, for them, it's in the past.

I almost cheered when I read in *I Don't Know How You Do It*, what Kate Reddy struggled to say to her colleague who had just decided not to have children. Kate shuts out the noise of the airport and tries to think of what Emily and Ben mean to her, then she turns to Momo and says:

> *Children are the proof we've been here, Momo, they're where we go to when we die. They're the best thing and the most impossible thing but there's nothing else. You have to believe me. Life is a riddle and they are the answer. If there's any answer, it has to be them.*[12]

The psychologist and author Harriet Lerner touched another deeply familiar fibre when she wrote:

> *Kids are the best teachers of life's most profound spiritual lessons; that pain and suffering are as much a part of life as happiness and joy; that change and impermanence are all we can count on for sure; that we don't really run the show.*[13]

I felt a similar frisson when I read in an interview how Britain's Father of the Year, Bob Geldof, described raising kids: 'There's so much crap talked about bringing up a child. A f**king moron could do it. Morons do bring up their children. It's just endless love, endless patience, that's it'.[14]

Just endless love and endless patience, according to Geldof. A leap of faith, Cannold says. Proof we've been here, says Kate Reddy. Reminders that we don't run the show, says Harriet Lerner. Whether we like it or not, when we speak about having children, our language tips into old territory. It is the language of religion but most of us don't think of it as religion. Metaphysical maybe, other-worldly perhaps, but whatever it is, it comes from somewhere deep within, from sometime a long time ago. It takes us out of the world we know and into a place that's both familiar and strange. It's a leap into the unknown in a world that wears safety belts. Having children is traditionally thought to be a conservative thing to do, but I think it is now a radical thing to do. When you decide to have children, you step outside the dominant culture; it is a snub to the culture of over-work, endless consumption and the pursuit of individual self-fulfilment. Having children throws us out of the rational world and counts us among the rash, the risk-takers and the dreamers.

Notes

Introduction

1   Kotlikoff, Laurence, J. and Burns, Scott, *The Coming Generational Storm*, The MIT Press, Cambridge, Massachusetts, 2004.

Chapter 1   The future is the past

1   Australian Bureau of Statistics, Australian Demographic statistics (3101.0); Population Projections, Australia (3222.0). Published in 2004 *Year Book Australia*, p. 87.

2   Turnbull, Malcolm, 'Is the West Dying Out: Family fertility and survival', Warrane Lecture 2003, University of NSW, Sydney, October 2003.

3   Tuchman, Barbara, *A Distant Mirror*, Penguin Australia, Victoria, 1980, p. 119.

4   McDonald, Peter, 'Low Fertility: Unifying the theory and the demography', a departmental technical report presented to Session 73, Future of Fertility in Low Fertility Countries at the 2002 meeting of the Population Association of America, Atlanta, May 2002, http://demography.anu.edu.au/Publications/PAA%20Paper%202002.doc.

5   Qu, Lixia, Weston, Ruth, Parker, Robin, 'Two to Tango? The importance of partnerships and partners' views in shaping fertility aspirations and expectations', unpublished paper, Australian Institute of Family Studies, presented to the Australian Social Policy Conference, University of NSW, Sydney, July 2003.

6   McDonald, Peter, 'Low Fertility: Unifying the theory and the demography'.

Chapter 2   The bionic woman

1   Norman, Robert, University of Adelaide Reproductive Medicine Unit, interview with author, April, 2004.

2   Lohrey, Amanda, The Philosopher's Doll, Penguin Group Australia, Melbourne, 2004.

3   Norman, Robert, interview with author, April, 2004.

4   Kimberley-Smith, Jo, 'Investigating the Impact of Perceptions of Assisted Reproductive Technology on the Decision to Delay Reproduction', University of Western Australia School of Anatomy and Human Biology, paper presented to Fertility Society of Australia Annual Scientific Meeting, Perth, November 2003.

5   Jansen, Robert, 'The Effect of Female Age on the Liklihood of a Live Birth from One In-vitro Fertilisation Treatment', Medical Journal of Australia, 2003 178(6): 258–261.

6   New Scientist, 'Test to Predict Menopause Revealed', 17 June, 2004.

7   Clark, Anne, medical director Sydney's Fertility First clinic, interview with author, May, 2004.

8   Norman, Robert, interview with author, April, 2004.

9   Pollard, Ruth, 'The "In Control" Generation is About to Lose It', Sydney Morning Herald, 2 February, 2003, p. 4.

10   Cannold, Leslie, 'Do We Need a Normative Account of the Decision to Parent?', Centre for Applied Philosophy and Public Ethics, Melbourne, Working Paper Number 2002/4.

11   Wolf, Naomi, Misconceptions: Truth, lies and the unexpected on the journey to motherhood, Chatto & Windus, London, 2001, p. 1.

Chapter 3   Ideology's orphan

1   Friedan, Betty, *The Feminine Mystique*, Victor Gollancz, London, 1971, p. 69.
2   Haussegger, Virginia, 'The Sins of Our Feminist Mothers', *Age*, 23 July, 2002, p. 11.
3   Summers, Anne, *Damned Whores and God's Police*, revised edition, Penguin Books, Australia, Melbourne, 2002, p. 17.
4   Millett, Kate, *Sexual Politics*, Granada, London, 1970, p. 23.
5   Engels, quoted in Greer, Germaine, *The Female Eunuch*, Harper Collins, London, 1993, p. 247.
6   Friedan, Betty, *The Feminine Mystique*, Victor Gollancz, London, 1971, pp. 75, 344.
7   Greer, Germaine, *The Female Eunuch*, p. 14.
8   Lake, Marilyn, *Getting Equal*, Allen & Unwin, Sydney, 1999, pp. 214, 217.
9   Greer, Germaine, *The Female Eunuch*, p. 262.
10 Bernard, Jessie, *The Future of Motherhood*, Penguin, New York, 1974.
11 Reiger, Kerreen, *Our Bodies Our Babies: The forgotten women's movement*, Melbourne University Press, Melbourne, 2001 p. 285.
12 Kitzinger, Sheila, *Ourselves as Mothers*, Transworld, Australia, Sydney, 1992, p. 5.
13 Leach, Penelope, *Children First*, Penguin Books, London, 1994, p. 35.
14 Bail, Kathy, *DIY Feminism*, Allen & Unwin, Sydney, 1996.
15 Maushart, Susan, *The Mask of Motherhood*, Random House Australia, Sydney, 1997, p. 314.
16 Summers, Anne, *The End of Equality*, Random House, 2003, p. 41.
17 Moore, Susan and David, *Child-Free Zone*, Chequered Gecko, Sydney, 2000.
18 Ehrlich, Paul and Anne, *The Population Explosion*, Simon & Schuster, New York, 1990, pp. 228–9.
19 McDonald, Peter, 'Understanding Australia's Population Dynamics', paper, www.science.org.au/proceedings/fenner/pdfs/PeterMcDonaldResponse.pdf.
20 Hollander, Jack M., *The Real Environmental Crisis*, University of California Press, Berkeley, 2003, p. 37.
21 Abbasi-Shavazi, Mohammad Jalal and Jones, Gavin (2001) 'Socio-economic and demographic setting of Muslim populations', *Technical Report Working Papers in Demography* no. 86, Demography and Sociology Program, RSSS, Australian National University, Canberra, 2002.
22 *Letter to the Bishops of the Catholic Church on the Collaboration of Men and Women in the Church and in the World*, 1 August, 2004, www.vatican.va/

roman_curia/congregations/cfaith/documents/rc_con_cfaith_doc_20040731
_collaboration_en.html.

23   Longman, Phillip, *The Empty Cradle*, Basic Books, New York, 2004, p. 35.

Chapter 4   Capitalism's child

1   Russell, Graeme and Hwang, Philip, 'The Impact of Workplace Practices
     on Fathering Involvement', *The Role of the Father in Child Development*, Wiley,
     New York, 2003.

2   Bittman, Michael and Pixley, Jocelyn, *The Double Life of the Family: Myth, hope
     and experience*, Allen & Unwin, Sydney, 1997, pp. 197, 198.

3   Pearson, Allison, *I Don't Know How She Does It*, Chatto and Windus, London,
     2002, p. 230.

4   Pocock, Barbara, *The Work/Life Collision*, The Federation Press, Sydney, 2003,
     p. 1.

5   Pearson, Allison, *I Don't Know How She Does It*, p. 104.

6   'The Household, Income and Labour Dynamics in Australia (HILDA) Survey',
     Department of Family and Community Services Annual Report, 2003.

7   Pocock, Barbara, *The Work/Life Collision*, p. 167.

8   Trinca, Helen and Fox, Catherine, *Better Than Sex: How a whole generation got
     hooked on work*, Random House, Sydney, 2004, p. 118.

9   Birrell, Bob, Rapson, Virginia and Hourigan, Clare, 'Men and Women
     Apart: The Decline of Partnering in Australia', Study prepared in the
     Monash University Centre for Population and Urban Research for the
     Australian Family Association, March, 2004.

10   De Laat, Joost, Sevilla-Sanz, Almudena, 'Working Women, Men's Time and
     Lowest–Low Fertility in Europe', Department of Economics, Brown
     University, August 2004, www.econ.brown.edu/"asanz/thesis/genderole.pdf.

11   Hochschild, Arlie, *The Time Bind: When work becomes home and home becomes
     work*, Metropolitan Books, New York, 1997.

12   Pocock, Barbara, *The Work/Life Collision*, Federation Press, Sydney, p. 52.

13   *HR Monthly*, Australian Human Resources Institute, Melbourne, June 2004
     issue.

14   Trinca, Helen and Fox, Catherine, *Better Than Sex: How a whole generation got
     hooked on work*, Random House, Sydney, 2004, p. 11.

15   Pearson, Allison, *I Don't Know How She Does It*, p. 51.

16   Hochschild, Arlie, *The Commercialisation of Intimate Life*, University of California Press, Berkeley, 2003.
17   Wolf, Naomi, *Misconceptions*, Chatto and Windus, London, 2001, p. 194.
18   Leach, Penelope, *Children First*, Penguin Books, London, 1994, p. 22.

Chapter 5   Home alone

1   'Profile of Young Australians', commissioned by Foundation for Young Australians, March 2004, www.youngaustralians.org/profile/home.htm.
2   Gilding Michael, 'Changing Families in Australia, 1901–2001', Australian Institute of Family Studies, *Family Matters* no. 60, Spring/Summer 2001.
3   Weston, Ruth, Qu, Lixia, 'Changing Patterns of Relationship Formation', unpublished paper for the Australian Institute of Family Studies, presented at the Australia-New Zealand Population Workshop, Canberra, 28–30 November, 2001.
4   Mackay, Hugh, *Generations: Baby boomers, their parents and their children*, Pan Macmillan Australia, Sydney, 1997, p. 151.
5   Macken, Deirdre, 'Hooking Up Not Getting Hitched', *Australian Financial Review*, 1 February, 2003.
6   Wyn, Johanna and White, Rob, *Youth and Society: Exploring the social dynamics of youth experience*, Oxford University Press, Melbourne, 2004, p. 4.
7   Lahdenpera, Mirkka, 'Fitness Benefits of Prolonged Post-reproductive Lifespan in Women', *Nature* magazine, 428, 11 March 2004, pp. 178–81.
8&9   Birrell, Bob, Rapson, Virginia and Hourigan, Clare, 'Men and Women Apart: The Decline of Partnering in Australia', study prepared in the Monash University Centre for Population and urban Research for the Australian Family Association, March, 2004.
10   Gilding, Michael, 'Changing Families in Australia, 1901–2001', Australian Institute of Family Studies, *Family Matters* no. 60, Spring/Summer 2001.

Chapter 6   Carefree singles and careless parents

1   Epstein, Joseph, 'The Perpetual Adolescent', *Weekly Standard*, 15 March, 2004, vol. 009, Issue 26.

2 Florida, Richard, *The Rise of the Creative Class: And how it's transforming work, leisure, community and everyday life*, Basic Books, New York, 2002.

3 Stalnaker, Stan, *Hub Culture: The next wave of urban consumers*, John Wiley, Singapore, 2002, pp. 3, 12, 13.

4 Watters, Ethan, *Urban Tribes: A generation redefines friendship, family and commitment*, Bloomsbury, New York, 2003.

5 Wyn, Johanna, interview with author, June, 2004.

6 Gladwell, Malcolm, *The Tipping Point: How little things can make a big difference*, Little Brown and Co, London, 2000.

7 *The Simpsons*, Series 15, Episode 8, 'Marge Vs Singles, Seniors, Childless Couples & Teens & Gays'.

8 Moore, Susan and David, *Child-Free Zone*, Chequered Gecko, Sydney, 2000.

9 Ladd-Taylor, Molly and Umansky, Lauri, *Bad Mothers: The politics of blame in twentieth-century America*, New York University Press, New York, 1997.

10 Kitzinger, Sheila, *Ourselves as Mothers*, Transworld Australia, Sydney, 1992, p. 8.

11 Pocock, Barbara, *The Work/Life Collision*, Federation Press, Sydney, p. 98.

12 Geldof, Bob, 'Bob Almighty', *Australian Women's Weekly*, April 2004.

13 Douglas, Susan and Michaels, Meredith, *The Mommy Myth: The idealisation of motherhood and how it has undermined women*, Simon & Schuster, New York, 2004.

Chapter 7 Children: All work, no play

1 Kitzinger, Sheila, *Ourselves as Mothers*, Transworld Australia, Sydney, p. 3.

2 NATSEM (National Centre for Social Economic Modelling) *Income and Wealth Report*, Issue 3, Canberra, October 2002.

3 Craig, Lyn and Bittman, Michael, 'The Time Costs of Children in Australia', unpublished paper, University of NSW Social Policy Research Centre, Sydney.

4 Longman, Phillip, 'Raising Hell, How the Punishing Costs of Childrearing Imperil Us All', *Washington Monthly*, March, 2004.

5 Ariès, Philippe, *Centuries of Childhood: A social history of family life*, Vintage Books, London, 1960, pp. 411, 412.

6 Fowler, F, 'The Ragged, Unruly and Unchaste', *Australian Childhood: An anthology*, (eds) Gwyn Dow and June Factor, McPhee Gribble, Melbourne, 1991, p. 77.

7   Bittman, Michael and Pixley, Jocelyn, *The Double Life of the Family: Myth, hope and experience*, Allen & Unwin, Sydney, 1997, pp. 189, 197–8.

8   Burggraf, Shirley, quoted in Longman, *The Empty Cradle*, Basic Books, New York, 2004, p. 142.

9   Leunig, Michael, 'Thoughts of a Baby Lying in a Child Care Centre' cartoon, *Age*, 29 July, 1995.

10 Macken, Deirdre, 'Drawing Blood', *Sydney Morning Herald*, 5 August, 1995.

11 Rayner, Moira, 'Leunig's Lonely Baby is Learning the Bleak Facts of Life!', *Age*, 31 July, 1995.

12 Margetts, Kay, 'Child Care Arrangements: Personal, family and school influences on children's adjustment to the first year of schooling', Faculty of Education, University of Melbourne, *Journal of Australian Research in Childhood Education*, 10(2), 2003.

13 Leslie, Careen, University of Canberra, Wiradjuri Centre, interview with author, June, 2004.

14 Leach, Penelope, *Children First*, Penguin Books, London, 1994, pp. 21, 22.

15 Leslie, Careen, interview with author, June, 2004.

16 Jarrell, Randall, Introduction to Christina Stead's *The Man Who Loved Children*, Angus & Robertson Publishers, Australian Classics edition, Sydney, 1979, p. xxvi.

Chapter 8   Myths, lies and masks

1   Williams, Zoe, 'You'll Understand Once You Have Kids . . .' , *Good Weekend Magazine, Sydney Morning Herald*, 14 February, 2004.

2   Wolf, Naomi, *Misconceptions*, Chatto and Windus, London, 2001, p. 217.

3   Lerner, Harriet, *The Mother Dance*, Harper Collins, New York, 1998, p. 53.

4   Maushart, Susan, *The Mask of Motherhood*, Random House, Australia, Sydney, p. 3.

5   Lerner, Harriet, *The Mother Dance*, p. 310.

6   De Laat, Joost, Sevilla-Sanz, Almudena, 'Working Women, Men's Home Time and Lowest-Low Fertility in Europe', Department of Economics, Brown University, August, 2004, www.econ.brown.edu/~asanz/thesis/genderole.pdf.

Chapter 9   No dogs, no children

1   Atwood, Margaret, *The Handmaid's Tale*, Virago Press, London, 1987, p. 1.
2   Tuchman, Barbara, *A Distant Mirror*, Penguin Australia, Victoria, 1980, p. 123.
3   McDonald, Peter, demographer, Australian National University, interview with author, May, 2004.
4   Goldstein, Joshua, Wolfgang, Lutz, Testa, Maria Rita, 'The Decline of Family Size Preference in Europe: Towards sub-replacement levels?', European Demographic Research Papers, 28 July 2004, www.oeaw.ac.at/vid/publications/EDRP.No2.pdf.
5   McDonald, Peter, interview with author, May, 2004.
6   Weston, Ruth, Australian Institute of Family Studies, interview with author, June, 2004.
7   Bagavos, Christos and Martin, Claude, 'Sinking Birth Rates, Family Structures and Political Reactions: Synthesis report', Annual convention Austrian Institute of Family Studies, Seville, Spain, 15–16 September, 2000.
8   McDonald, Peter, interview with author, May, 2004.
9   Wyn, Johanna, director, Youth Research Centre, University of Melbourne, interview with author, July, 2004.

Chapter 10   The lie of the land

1   Longman, Phillip, *The Empty Cradle: How falling birthrates threaten world prosperity and what to do about it*, Basic Books, New York, 2004, Ch. 9.
2   McDonald, Peter, demographer, Australian National University, interview with author, May 2004.
3   *Intergenerational Report*, Australian Treasury, Canberra, 2002.
4   Florida, Richard, *The Rise of the Creative Class: And how it's transforming work, leisure, community and everyday life*, Basic Books, New York, 2002.
5   Landler, Mark, 'East Germany Swallows Billions and Still Stagnates', *New York Times*, 21 July, 2004.
6   *2003 State of the Regions Report*, National Economics and Australian Local Government Association, www.alga.asn.au/policy/regional/2003sor.php.

7   Macken, Deirdre, 'We Shall Fight Them on the Beaches', *Australian Financial Review*, 29 November, 2003.
8   Hugo, Graeme, Department of Geography, Adelaide University, interview with author, March, 2004.

Chapter 11   Knitting bootees for the country

1   'Valuing Parenthood: Options for Paid Maternity Leave', Interim Paper, Human Rights and Equal Opportunity Commission, Sydney, 2002.
2   Letablier, Marie-Thérèse, 'Fertility and Family Policies in France', *Journal of Population and Social Security* (Population) Supplement to Volume 1 (now the *Japanese Journal of Population*), www.ipss.go.jp/English/WebJournal.files?population/pso3-6.html.
3   Clinton, Hillary Rodham, *It Takes a Village*, Simon & Schuster, New York, 1996, p. 223.
4   Clinton, Hillary Rodham, *It Takes a Village*, p. 288.
5   Durie, John, '2004: The view from the top', *Australian Financial Review*, 31 December, 2003.
6   Longman, Phillip, *The Empty Cradle*, Basic Books, New York, 2004, Ch. 12.
7   Quoted in Nancarrow, Kate, 'Father Time', *Age*, 23 May, 2004.
8   Russell, Graeme and Hwang, Philip, 'The Impact of Workplace Practices on Father Involvement', in Lamb, M.E. *The Role of the Father in Child Development*, Wiley, New York, 2003.
9   Watson, Don, *Death Sentence*, Random House, Sydney, 2003.
10 De Marneffe, Daphne, *Maternal Desire*, Little Brown and Co, New York, 2004, pp. 11, 13.
11 Cannold, Leslie, interview with author, August, 2004.
12 Pearson, Allison, *I Don't Know How She Does It*, Chatto and Windus, London, 2003, p. 165.
13 Lerner, Harriet, *The Mother Dance*, Harper Collins, London, 1998, p. 310.
14 Geldof, Bob, 'Bob Almighty', *Australian Women's Weekly*, April, 2004.

Index